MW00775282

At David C Cook, we equip the local church around the corner and around the globe to make disciples. Come see how we are working together—go to **www.davidccook.org**. Thank you!

transforming lives together

Rest

A **THRIVE**MOMS BIBLE STUDY

Rest

FINDING STILLNESS IN THE MIDST OF BUSY

Kara-Kae James
& Ali Pedersen

DAVID C COOK

transforming lives together

REST
Published by David C Cook
4050 Lee Vance Drive
Colorado Springs, CO 80918 U.S.A.

Integrity Music Limited, a Division of David C Cook
Brighton, East Sussex BN1 2RE, England

The graphic circle C logo is a registered trademark of David C Cook.

The website addresses recommended throughout this book
are offered as a resource to you. These websites are not
intended in any way to be or imply an endorsement on the
part of David C Cook, nor do we vouch for their content.

ISBN 978-0-8307-7311-4
eISBN 978-0-8307-7914-7

The Author is represented by Alive Literary
Agency, 7680 Goddard Street, Suite 200, Colorado
Springs, CO 80920, www.aliveliterary.com.

Cowritten by Ali Pedersen
The Team: Alice Crider, Laura Derico, Amy Konyndyk,
Nick Lee, Jack Campbell, Susan Murdock
Cover Design: Jon Middel

Printed in the United States of America
First Edition 2019

1 2 3 4 5 6 7 8 9 10

061919

CONTENTS

HOW TO USE THIS STUDY

Before you turn to the study pages, sit for a moment with this question: What do you hope to get out of this study? (Write your answer below.)

Welcome to this Thrive Moms Bible study! Thrive Moms (www.thrivemoms.com) is a ministry that exists to encourage and inspire moms everywhere to do more than just *survive* motherhood. We want you to thrive, and we believe thriving happens when you connect with God's Word and one another.

This Bible study can be done as an individual or with a group. But we know we are always better together! Even if you grab just one friend to walk through the study with you, you'll stay on track better and keep each other accountable.

There are six weeks of study, and each week has four days (to not overwhelm you). Do these day studies at the times that work best for you. Each study week includes these features:

- Go to the Word sections to offer specific Bible verses to focus on.
- Simple questions to help you process the Bible passages.

- Space provided for you to make your own connections.
- Prayer suggestions to lead into your personal time with God.

Each week wraps up with a group discussion option, designed to offer time to talk over what you've learned from God's Word through the week, to share your experiences, and to learn from and encourage one another.

Prepare yourself with time and accountability as you begin. We will be praying for you as you search for stillness and find rest in the Lord!

GROUP DISCUSSION GROUND RULES
SAFE SPACE
You are entering a safe space here, and it will all be worth it. Allow yourself to break down some walls and trust the women God has placed around you. Be honest and trustworthy with others. A key part of your personal growth is found in community with others. Be intentional in your conversation and the way you process Scripture.

COMMITMENT
Commit to do the work! We have made the study sessions intentionally short so that they are not overly time consuming. (They were written for busy moms!) Whether you are doing the study on your own, with a friend, or with a group, make the commitment to attend and be involved. You'll get the most out of this study if you commit to it. The curriculum is not overwhelming, so there are no excuses!

DISCUSSION

When talking in a group, be concise with your answers. Remember that everyone's time is precious, and everyone should have an opportunity to speak. What happens in the group, stays in the group. Keep discussion confidential. Scripture is our basis for everything. We may be drawn to giving worldly advice, but the best truth is God's!

If you are leading a group, see more tips for leaders at the end of this book in the Leader Guide.

WHY REST?

Rest. Our bodies crave it. Our souls cry out for it. But it's the one thing we battle the most to fit into our overwhelmed days and schedules. We've always found the story of Jesus resting on the boat in Mark 4:35–40 a bit intriguing. It's kind of nice seeing the human, and slightly dramatic, side of the disciples:

> On that day, when evening had come, he told them, "Let's cross over to the other side of the sea." So they left the crowd and took him along since he was in the boat. And other boats were with him. A great windstorm arose, and the waves were breaking over the boat, so that the boat was already being swamped. He was in the stern, sleeping on the cushion. So they woke him up and said to him, "Teacher! Don't you care that we're going to die?"
>
> He got up, rebuked the wind, and said to the sea, "Silence! Be still!" The wind ceased, and there was a great calm. Then he said to them, "Why are you afraid? Do you still have no faith?"

Notice that the water was already coming into the boat, but somehow Jesus was able to sleep through it all until the disciples woke Him up, accusing Him of not caring if the boat sank and they all died. We believe Jesus knew exactly what was going on and what He was doing, and that this story contains a great teaching moment for us all. Jesus had spent the day teaching to crowds of people, and He knew it was time to stop and rest ... even though there was a storm brewing.

If Jesus can find the time in the midst of a storm to take a nap, we can too, friend. He knew what He and the disciples were about to face, and the Son of God still rested.

We moms can feel guilty when we take time to rest physically, mentally, or emotionally, because so many things are screaming for our attention. But God knows when we need to give our bodies, minds, and hearts a break. In Psalm 127:2 we read, "In vain you rise early and stay up late, toiling for food to eat—for he grants sleep to those he loves" (NIV).

We need to stop feeling guilty about rest and start leaning into the importance of filling our soul with the refreshment God has for us. When we rest, we are able to give back so much more to our people who need us. We can't pour from an empty vessel, yet that's what so many of us are trying to do. We pour and pour until we are completely dry, and then we can't figure out why we have nothing left to give.

It's time to rest and fill back up. Put the guilt aside—and for the love, take a nap if you need one! Rest in the Lord. Find stillness, and stop running on empty.

WHAT DOES IT MEAN TO REST IN THE LORD?

You know that feeling of relief that washes over you at the end of the day, when you fall into bed? The kids are asleep, the day's tasks done, and you can finally take a deep breath and sink into your pillow. An almost tingly sensation runs through your body as the stress and tension melt away, if only for a short time (before a child comes wandering out of bed).

That is how I imagine resting in the Lord. A retreat from the demands of this world. The noise of the day traded for quiet. A time when I can hear that still, small voice speaking straight to my heart. The Father cradling my weary body as I sink into the warmth and safety of His arms.

Throughout the Bible we see many commands: be still, wait on the Lord, be anxious for nothing, fear not. The Lord wants us to find peace and rest in Him—a safe space to recharge when the world takes the best of what we have to offer. Psalm 131:1–2 says, "O LORD, my heart is not lifted up; my eyes are not raised too high; I do not occupy myself with things too great and too marvelous for me. But I have calmed and quieted my soul, like a weaned child with its mother; like a weaned child is my soul within me" (ESV). We are called to a quiet obedience. When we submit ourselves to this practice of rest, we are allowing our hearts and minds the space and freedom to glean the truth and wisdom the Father has for us.

Day One

REST IN THE LORD

Exodus 20:8–11; 31:12–15; Psalm 37:5–7; Hebrews 1:3

For many of us, sleep is a rare commodity—as precious as that last pound of coffee beans on the grocery store shelf. I often wake up in the early morning to find myself teetering on the edge of my bed with multiple children lying on top of me. It's not super relaxing. With early feedings, late-night consoling, morning workouts, afternoon playdates, doctors' appointments, sports meets, and work meetings, the schedule of a mom has everything included except a moment to breathe. There is typically not time for a nap. Thankfully, resting in the Lord doesn't require actual sleep!

So, what does it really mean to rest in the Lord?

Rest is a very big idea in the Old Testament. From the very beginning, Yahweh makes the idea of rest a high ideal. On the seventh day, God initiates rest for the first time. It's the concept of ceasing from work, but it's also about completion.

Go to the Word: Read Exodus 20:8–11.

Looking at verse 10, who in Israel does the Lord expect to keep the law of the Sabbath?

What does that tell you about the importance of this to God?

 ✍️ **Go to the Word:** *Read Exodus 31:12–15.*

The Lord definitely takes this idea seriously. Looking in verse 13, God wants them to observe the Sabbath as a sign for two reasons.

Write those two reasons in the space provided.

With the Sabbath being established in the Law, the Lord clearly sees this principle of completing work and resting to be important enough that every person, regardless of status, should be reminded to rest every week. *Sabbath* means "seven" in Hebrew, but the number has become synonymous with resting. The Lord designed our very concept of a week as a reminder to rest. When work is complete, we rest. As humans, it is expected that we do need time to rest and refuel in order to function—we definitely feel it when we lack the rest we need.

Yet for some reason, some people (both Christians and people in other religions, or even people with no religion at all) claim that God wants people to fulfill works to please Him. One view is that after death God looks at the wrong you've done and then compares it with the weight of the good done. The idea is that bad can be overcome with the accomplishment of good. Work can overcome shortcoming. What we actually see from the Lord is something different.

⮕ **Go to the Word:** *Read Psalm 37:5-7.*

From verse 5, who is the one who will act or do something?

In verse 7, instead of working harder, what does David write that we should do before the Lord?

The Lord is wanting His followers to understand that there is no amount of work or actions or good deeds that can overcome the evil that is accomplished. Our justification before God does not come from the works we do. Our righteousness is not created by acts of our hands. Our salvation does not come through sweat. Instead, God wants His disciples to commit our hearts to Him, to trust Him, to wait for Him—He will accomplish the justifying, will be the righteousness, and will do the saving.

Go to the Word: *Read Hebrews 1:3.*

According to this verse, what did Jesus do once the work of purification had been finished?

Once the work was completed, Jesus sat down at the right hand of the Father. The work had been accomplished, and so He sat. He rested. There was nothing else to be done. So, sisters, if Jesus has rested from the work of salvation, why should we continue to strive to accomplish the same work? Sit down. We can rest in Him. We don't need to keep trying to measure up. We don't have to account for, work for, accomplish, or finish anything in order to receive salvation. Either the work Jesus accomplished is enough, or it isn't. Either the purification for sins is complete, or it isn't. We could never be enough, but Jesus is enough.

How do we show our faith in His finished work and believe it is enough to cover our sins? Rest. Rest in Him. Trust that His work done on your behalf is actually good enough. Truthfully, if the work of the Son of God was not enough, what would make us think that our imperfect works could be of any help? Trust in Him. Rest in Him and wait expectantly for His salvation to work in our lives, producing righteousness.

PRAYER FOR REST

During this study, use these prayer times as small Sabbath moments—time to rest for even just a few minutes from whatever chaos your day might bring or has brought you already. Go back and pick one of the scriptures to focus on. Read over it several times, remembering these are God's words for you. Thank God for speaking with you this way.

Day Two

OUR JOY MADE COMPLETE
John 15:1–11

Have you ever been away from home for a long time, long enough to really miss it? Once you are home, you experience a sense of real completeness. The people you love, the familiar settings, even the smells that surround you, they all make you feel at home.

When we are where we belong, it makes us want to stay. Whenever I travel, I enjoy the freedom for a day or two, but beyond that, I just miss home. Home is a place of belonging, where all the little people who love me reside. Coming home to them makes me feel complete.

In John 15, Jesus uses the picture of a vine and its branches. Just as we learned in first grade, when we watched little beans grow into sprouts, in order for all parts of the plant to grow, they need to connect, and all the parts need to remain. If you tear off a leaf, it will wither and die.

✐ **Go to the Word:** *Read John 15:1–8.*

What does Jesus call Himself?

What does Jesus call His disciples?

What does Jesus say anyone in Him does?

Jesus states that the key to producing fruit is remaining or residing in Him. In fact, He repeats that idea several times in this passage. If we are going to bear fruit, we need to reside in Him. If we separate from Jesus, we will not bear fruit.

What does Jesus state will happen to a branch that does not remain in the vine?

Go to the Word: Read John 15:9–11.

How can we stay in Jesus' love?

Why does Jesus say He has told us all of this?

Jesus says we can have complete joy. But the key to how to have this joy is for us to remain where we belong; we need to reside at home. And Jesus is our home! This is where we find complete joy.

For us who are redeemed by Jesus, He is our connection to life. To be "in Him" means we are connected to the source of our new life, our eternal life. We are new creations in Jesus, and to live out this new life, we need to live the way God designed us to live.

Joy is connected with the love of God, and the love of God is connected with obedience. Not that God only loves us when we obey, but that we understand His love more when we obey His commands. Just as any good parent does for a child, our Father gives us commands *because* He loves us. As Romans 13:10 puts it, "Love, therefore, is the fulfillment of the law." We show where we reside by our behavior. We show who we love and follow by our actions. Like a connected branch in the vine shows its health by growing fruit—we show we are residing in Jesus by what we produce. When we are at home where we are intended to reside, growing as we are intended to grow, this is where we truly find our joy.

As a parent, how does the idea of joy in relation to obedience resonate with you?

How can we show obedience to the Lord and at the same time find joy? When does that seem like a struggle?

Joy is defined in *Webster's Dictionary* (from 1828) in this way: "Joy is a delight of the mind, from the consideration of the present or assured approaching possession of a good." I think it is safe to say that in our modern culture we have a skewed view of what happiness is, and we definitely need to recalibrate what joy means.

In considering our future with Jesus in heaven, ruling with Him, receiving understanding, and experiencing all that heaven has to offer, our delight in that should bring us joy. Whatever we are currently experiencing, being assured of an overabundance of blessing in the future allows us to have joy in our present circumstance. Being found in Jesus, resting and residing in Him, means that we are never separated from His blessing. Even here on earth we live as a vine in the branch. We receive our eternal quality life from Him now through the understanding of His plan for us. We have the promise of future eternal life and blessings forever with Him.

By living in His love now, we can experience that full and complete joy now. Are you discouraged today? Remember what He has given you through His Word. Do you know someone who is in a time of despair? We can find that complete joy in Jesus now and have enough to share with others. Outside of Jesus, there is no hope for the future. Give freely of the complete joy that you have!

PRAYER FOR REST

Take a Sabbath moment to remember one of the last times you felt joy. Look through some photos that remind you of that time, or just bring up a mental image of what was happening then. Thank God for glimpses of joy we have here now, and ask Him to help you hold on tight to the hope of heaven and eternal life with Him, so you can experience joy even in difficult circumstances.

Day Three

ENTERING INTO GOD'S REST
Matthew 11:28–30; 12:1–8; Genesis 3:8–13

Have you ever trained for a race? A 5k perhaps, or even a 10k? Maybe a half marathon or, if you are a real overachiever, a full marathon! Those first few days and weeks of training are rough. Every little muscle in your legs hurts, and you have to find it in yourself to go back out and run again the next day. I know for me, I struggle with trying to run for the whole race. Everything in me wants to stop and walk. So, I look ahead down the path or trail and choose a point, a landmark of some kind, and I tell myself, "Okay, you just have to get to that spot!" And then I keep running. When I get there, I look down the path once again and choose a new goal, and another and another and another, until the race is complete and I have made it to the end!

What is it that makes running a race SO hard and SO exhausting? It is the burden of our own bodies! Having to carry the weight of ourselves for miles and miles, when all we want to do is sit down and release the burden.

Go to the Word: Read Matthew 11:28–30.

In your own words, what do you think this yoke or burden that Jesus talks about is? What are we supposed to take up from Him?

Jesus invites those who are weary to take on His burden. Who are the weary?

If Jesus' burden is light, then the burden of the weary by contrast must be heavy. Why is their burden heavy? What makes a burden hard to carry?

 Go to the Word: *Read Matthew 12:1-8.*

What example did Jesus give to teach about the Sabbath?

According to verse 7, what did Jesus say He desires more than sacrifice?

Write out verse 8 in the space below.

In verse 8, Jesus states that the Son of Man is the Lord of the Sabbath, but what does that mean? The perspective of the Pharisees and experts in the Law was that there was a list of things to do (or in this case, not to do) to show that they were righteous or holy in their observance of the Sabbath. But Jesus pointed out that, by focusing on their rules, they actually had misunderstood God's intention for the Sabbath.

In the example Jesus used, David and his men were hungry to the point of fainting. Seeing them in this state, the priest fed them the only readily available bread, which was the bread in the holy place in the tabernacle. Jesus also pointed out that priests still do priestly work on the Sabbath, and yet the Lord does not count this as violating the Sabbath.

The Sabbath was not made to be a burden for people. The Sabbath was meant to give rest. It was meant to lead people toward the promised respite from the burdens of work. With their additional requirements, the Pharisees had changed the Sabbath from a time for rest, and a promise to look forward to, into just another kind of work.

Let's look at Matthew 11:28–30 again. Remember those weary and burdened people Jesus talked about? That kind of burden comes from trying to achieve your own righteousness. Working to make a relationship right is the heaviest of burdens, especially when that relationship is with the Creator of the universe, who holds the keys to eternal life.

⟋⟋ **Go to the Word:** *Read Genesis 3:8–13.*

Instead of eagerly anticipating an experience of the Lord, what emotion did Adam and Eve feel when they heard God in the garden?

What did Adam give as the reason for hiding from God?

Considering Adam's response in verse 12, how might you describe the relationship between man and woman after the Fall—after they first sinned by disobeying God?

Having a right relationship with God is what has been missing since Adam and Eve first ate from the forbidden tree. When sin entered the world, humans lost that right relationship with God. We could no longer walk with God and talk with Him. We were separated from Him because of our own choices. Since the Fall, every human has failed in a similar way. This right relationship between God the Father and His people is called righteousness. The burden to right this relationship is heavy. So heavy, in fact, that it weighs us down and keeps us from running the race of life in the way the Lord intended.

But Jesus offers us a way to lose this heavy weight—He offers us His burden instead. It's the burden of His righteousness.

This righteousness is perfect. Jesus has never been in rebellion before the Lord or had a broken relationship. His righteousness is complete—not lacking in any way. This righteousness is the work of Jesus. This is the work He completed on the cross. He proved it when He exited the grave in His resurrection. If we take on His burden, we can have a right relationship with God again. And because the work is completed, His burden is light and is a joy to carry. With the burden of Christ, we can all run and not ever be weary (Isaiah 40:31).

PRAYER FOR REST

Pretend Jesus is standing before you, inviting you to come and offering you rest for your soul. What do you want to say to Him?

Day Four
ABUNDANT LIFE
John 10:7–18; Matthew 6:25–27; 1 John 5:11–12

As moms, we are told we only have to hang on until bedtime. If you drink enough coffee, you'll make it through the day! Hide in the closet and treat yourself to some chocolate to preserve your sanity.

At times, coffee, chocolate, and closet hangs can get you through the day, but motherhood isn't about clinging to your sanity by your fingertips. It's not about wishing your kids were in bed or dreaming of the days you were kid-free. It's about enjoying the time while they are little. It's about appreciating them as they blossom into adulthood. It's about loving who they are as humans and who they are in Christ.

Motherhood isn't about survival; it's about thriving! Obviously every day won't be bliss—that would be ridiculous—but there is just so much abundance to be experienced in the short time you have with your kiddos. Similarly, we are called not only to survive in Christ but to live abundantly! We were not saved to live mediocre lives. He has saved us for His purposes and longs for us to participate fully in what He has in store for us.

Go to the Word: *Read John 10:7–10.*

What does Jesus call Himself in verse 7?

Who do you think Jesus is referring to in verse 8? Who were those that came before?

What three things does the thief come to do?

During the time when Jesus lived on earth, shepherds would often take their flocks to graze far away from a town or even a barn as we would think of it. During the night, they would hold their flocks in a simple stone enclosure with no gate or door. Once the sheep were safely inside, the shepherd would lie across the opening. The shepherd's body would act as the door.

When Jesus says He is the door or the gate, there are a few things He is teaching that would have been much more obvious to His disciples then, since this word picture reflected a familiar part of their culture. In this metaphor, Jesus, as the shepherd, protects the life of the sheep. Inside the enclosure, there are no sheep sweating in their sleep, uncertain of their safety. They know they are safe. All around them is an enclosure, and the only opening is guarded. The shepherd guards the lives of the sheep. The sheep trust the shepherd.

As the door, Jesus keeps those who are His from being lost. Jesus keeps the sheep from leaving. No sheep can simply wander past the shepherd and leave the enclosure. And Jesus, guarding the sheep, can easily identify any oncoming enemy.

 Go to the Word: *Read John 10:11–18.*

How would you describe the difference between the shepherd and the "hired hand"?

What does the good shepherd do for the sheep?

The good shepherd is invested in the sheep because they are his. The reason he protects them is because he cares about them. They are valuable to him. Every sheep matters.

When an enemy comes, the good shepherd doesn't run away. The hired hand values his life more than the sheep, so he leaves when he feels danger coming. But the good shepherd lays down his life for his sheep. That is how much he cares about them.

The sheep show their trust in the shepherd by simply resting. Their rest is the expression of their trust. And they trust the shepherd because they know him well. They know he will protect them.

This is exactly the same for us, the disciples of Jesus. The more we know Him, the more our trust in Him grows. We can rest in the knowledge that He will protect us and that He values each one of us. Unrest is a thief of joy, and anxiety is the enemy of faith.

Go to the Word: Read Matthew 6:25–27.

Complete this statement from verse 25: "Don't worry about ..."

"Don't worry about your life." That is such an amazing command! Write that down! Write it on the mirror in the bathroom, get a bumper sticker, or get a tattoo! This is one command you definitely want to remember word for word.

Write down verse 27 in your own words.

What do you think about Jesus' question? The implied answer is, of course, no. No, no one adds seconds to her life by worrying. But do our lives show that we believe that? Do we really live like we know that holding on to anxiety cannot do any good to change our circumstances?

✒ **Go to the Word:** *Read 1 John 5:11–12.*

Who has given eternal life, and where is it found?

What must someone have in order to have eternal life?

This eternal life is not just a life that goes on forever and doesn't end. The word used for "eternal" in this context gives the idea of a quality of life. It's a life free from chronic worry and free from the fear of judgment and condemnation. It's a life where we have a close relationship with Jesus, walking with Him and talking with Him. It's a life where we can rest in Him. It's abundant life. And that life begins now: "The one who has the Son has life" (verse 12).

The life we have now is guarded by our Shepherd, and that life is an eternal-quality kind of life. But that life is found only in Jesus and nowhere else.

PRAYER FOR REST

In your Sabbath moment today, ponder the command "Don't worry about your life." Focus on just one small detail of your life that you often worry about. Ask God to help you release your concern or fears about that detail, and trust Him to provide what you need.

Group Discussion

STARTER

Talk about the last time you experienced real rest. Maybe it was on vacation, or because of a great nap, or even just five quiet minutes in the car by yourself.

REVIEW

1. After this week's study, what does resting in the Lord mean to you?

2. How can we begin to make a practice of resting in the Lord?

3. In what ways do you think the Lord is asking you to be obedient today? How might joy come with that obedience?

4. What burdens are you carrying that you need to lay down?

5. How is unrest or anxiety stealing your joy?

PRAYER FOR REST

Take a Sabbath moment together as a group. Let someone read Psalm 131:1–2 out loud. Then allow a few minutes of silence. Listen to the sounds around you. Listen to your own breathing. And listen to what you have heard from God's Word. Let God calm and quiet your souls. Close with a simple "Amen."

Room to Reflect

HOW KNOWING GOD BRINGS YOU REST

One of the key elements in stepping into rest is understanding the character of God. When we can better understand who He is, what His character looks like, and the truth about Him—we can become more like Him. And when we become more like Him, resting in the Lord becomes a more natural state of our lives.

This week we will camp out mostly in Psalms as we get a deeper understanding of God's character through the eyes of the psalm writers, hearing mostly from David. David's story is so fascinating because he was a sinner just like you and me—and still was chasing after God every step of the way. Through these psalms and a few pieces of the Old Testament, we will begin to understand more about who God is to us and how knowing Him better can bring us rest.

Our end goal is to become more like God, to lean into what He teaches us about ourselves and what He has for us. This week is our *why*. When we learn who God is, we begin to desire to seek rest only in Him. When we learn who God is, we naturally find that rest in Him. When we rest in Him and trust Him, we discover more about who and what He created us to be.

We can find rest in the Lord, because of who He is.

Rest

Day One

GOD IS WORTHY
Psalm 96

As we seek to understand who God is, we should first grasp why He is worthy of our worship. Let's take some time today to read through Psalm 96. This is a psalm written as a call to worship. The writer is declaring the reasons we should worship God. He asks people to sing praise to the Lord, and then he points out why.

✍ **Go to the Word:** _Read Psalm 96:1-6. Write out the reasons the author gives for worshipping God in verses 4-6._

One of my favorite words in the Bible is _but_, because you always know that after you read it, something good is coming. In verse 5, we see that all the other gods created by our hands are idols—_but_ the Lord is worthy because He's our Creator God. He made the heavens.

God can be described in many ways, and His list of positive character traits is long—we see some of those traits in this psalm.

What are some words that come to mind when you think of the character of God?

A few words I think of to describe God are *powerful, holy, just, righteous, forgiving, compassionate, wise, provider, creative* ... I could go on and on. There are so many incredible characteristics that tell us something about who God is. No matter where you look or how you describe God, He breaks all the molds. He will always be bigger and greater than we can grasp.

But even though we may know that God is worthy, we may not always *feel* like worshipping. Before I was married—and before kids—it seemed like I had so much time to study God's Word and learn about Him. I could close the door and, for hours, pore over the words He has given us. Now, as a mom with four kids, I'm lucky if I get five minutes alone. In my exhaustion, I don't always feel like worshipping God.

But worshipping God isn't about our *feelings*. This can be hard to get, especially when our emotions are running strong and we want to turn Scripture into what we want it to mean. But the truth is, we worship God and follow Him because He is worthy, not because we feel like it.

I went through a season recently when I just felt empty. It was hard and painful, and I felt like God was so far away. This sort of season was tough for David too, as he wrote in this psalm. His worship was tied in with the remembrance of God's faithfulness.

When you are struggling to see God's face and hear His voice—you can continue to worship in remembrance of His faithfulness. No matter how difficult this present season is for you, you can know that God has always been faithful!

✐ Go to the Word: *Read Psalm 96:10–13. Write out what the psalmist says God has done and will do.*

Think back to all the times God has come through and faithfully shown His character to you or to someone in your family or community. Write down some of those times God has shown up for you.

As moms, we often feel like our wells of energy have run dry. We are exhausted and weary. When you are experiencing this, don't lean into your feelings to find a reason to worship. Lean into the truth—into what you know about who God is and how He has shown His faithfulness to us. He is worthy, no matter where you are or how you feel. He is worthy because of who He is!

What is something that stands out to you in this psalm about God's character? Why is that aspect of God important to you?

PRAYER FOR REST

Take a moment to rest and worship the Lord God by praying this prayer: Lord, I worship You even when I don't feel like it. Let my life be a reflection of worship and praise to You, even in my exhaustion. Help me see ways that I can better understand and know Your character. Give me a remembrance of You that carries me through, even when I feel like I can't go on. Thank You for who You are and how I can grow to be more like You!

Day Two
GOD IS THE VOICE
Psalm 29

In Genesis, God's Word opens by saying He spoke everything into being. What a powerful voice to simply speak and have a universe appear! God created humankind, and at first, He could speak to man, and the man and woman had no shame or fear at the sound of the voice of the Lord. But after the man and woman sinned, they felt shame. And when they heard the sound of God walking in the garden, they did not go out to Him. Instead, they hid. Scripture tells us that God called out to the man, and the man confessed that he was afraid. He was afraid not of the sound of God's voice, but of the presence that voice represented (Genesis 3:8–11).

Go to the Word: *Read Psalm 29.*

In this psalm, we find beautiful imagery talking about the voice of the Lord and the power that comes with it. In ancient times, some cultures felt that the voices of their gods represented how much power they held. And these "voices" were often linked with sounds from nature—the sounds of weather or of various animals. Similarly in this psalm, each time we see "the voice" repeated, there's a description of God's power. But the difference here is that we are not the ones giving power to God through our descriptions of Him. He has all the power, and we struggle to represent that power through words. So we talk about Him shaking and breaking and flashing and making things with only the sound of His voice because we want to communicate the idea that God is so full of power, He doesn't even need to lift a finger to make things happen.

We hear so many times about how powerful God is. Why does it matter that we know God is powerful? How does knowing He is powerful affect us?

Write down some of the images from Psalm 29.

How should we be changed by seeing all of these attributes of God?

My kids have a bad habit of leaving their closet light on, which means we replace the light bulb every couple of months because it's always burning out. The problem is, the closet ceiling is high, and a ladder is required to reach the light. So, when the bulb does burn out, we are often slow to change it. During this lapse, the kids are afraid to go in the closet when it's dark, so they will ask me to walk in and get their clothes and shoes. Their worried faces ease when I come back out of the closet—they are obviously relieved that I have not been eaten by a monster.

God's power is like this for us. When we find ourselves afraid to walk into the darkness, He goes before us. When everything is a bit scary and uneasy, He goes before us. He lets us hear His voice in Scripture, so we know how powerful He is. His power gives us the strength to face difficult situations in our lives. We know that He is in control and our circumstances are in His hands.

Fill in the blank. God's power gives me _____ _____.

We have no reason to fear, because God is the voice—the voice of power. His character over and over reminds us that He is above all and nothing is too big for Him. As followers of Christ, we should live with absolute peace. We are free from fear and shame and can walk with confidence (even through the dark) because of His voice!

Are you living like God's voice is powerful? What are some things that make it hard for you to walk confidently in your faith?

How do these things keep you from resting in the Lord?

PRAYER FOR REST

Read over Psalm 29 and use it as you pray: Lord, You are powerful! Help me to see and remember that today as I step into my tasks and also find rest in You. I am so thankful I can hear the power of Your voice.

Day Three
GOD IS FOR ALL
Psalm 71

I grew up with the belief that if I messed up, I was doomed. The Bible was a strict list of rules to me, most of which I didn't really understand. I did the "church thing" because I was supposed to, and following the rules felt right to my type A personality. Unfortunately, though, my relationship with God became a kind of checklist and a way to meet my obsessive need for perfection.

Has your relationship with God ever been like this? Explain a time in your life (maybe now!) that your relationship with God felt like a checklist.

I had to fall on my face a bit before I really began to understand more about who God is. What a relief it was to learn that He is not a dictator, but a grace-filled Father who wants nothing more than an intimate relationship with us!

We all crash and burn at some point, in one way or another. It's impossible to be a perfect mom for even one day, much less for our whole lives. But since we are all imperfect moms here, let's look closer at our perspectives on God from this season of our lives:

Go to the Word: Read Psalm 71:1–8.

Jot down some descriptions of God from this passage. Are these descriptions something you can relate to in some way? What do you learn from them?

In this psalm, we look at how God is a God for all generations. The writer here begins by talking about his perceptions of God from his youth and then moves into his thoughts from his old age and about passing on his knowledge to the next generation. The writer wants to make sure the generations to come know exactly who God is. He is our *rock*. He is our *fortress*. He is the safe place we can always go to find rest and refuge.

Our children will receive messages about what to believe from a thousand different directions—messages about who God is and who God should be to them. It's our responsibility to point them to the truth.

A lot of people see God as a stuffy dictator whom they can't even approach. Others think that God might be someone like their worship pastor, wearing skinny jeans and playing loud music (no judgment here; I'm happily married to a worship pastor!).

As humans, we are constantly changing. What we like from one year to the next changes. The way we worship and the songs we sing change. But there is One who stands constant throughout time—always there for us, always our strength, always ready to rescue us.

How have you viewed God for the majority of your life? Be honest! Place an *X* on the line below to show where your vision of God might fit.

Stuffy Dictator God   Cool, Skinny Jeans God   Grace-Giving Father God

←————————————————————————————→

What is your perspective of God right now? How would you describe your relationship with Him?

We simply cannot put God in our own little box. That's not who He is. He is God for us all—He meets us where we are. I have found God in an African village gathering, with no walls, no electricity, and no fancy light show. I've found God among thousands of people, with loud music blaring and deep, biblical teaching. I've met God in a country church, with a hymnal in my hand. I've met God in my minivan, surrounded by screaming kids. When we seek God, we will find Him, no matter where we are or what we think He is like.

Think about the places where God has met you. Write down a few of those places and how they have impacted your view of who God is.

It's our responsibility to carry on the truth about God to the next generation—not a God shaped to fit our opinions, but God as we see Him through His Word.

*☞ **Go to the Word:** Read Psalm 71:17–19.*

How can we proclaim God's power and strength to the next generation? Who can we rely on to teach us how to do this?

How are you portraying God to your children?

PRAYER FOR REST

Use the words of Psalm 71 to guide you as you pray today: Lord, I find rest in You today because You are unchanging. You are my refuge, my rock, my fortress. I find peace in knowing that You are steady and true. Help me to introduce You to my children as the God who You are and not just who I want You to be.

Day Four

WHO IS GOD?

Exodus 33–34; Psalm 103

Most of my life I had an extensive head knowledge of God, but developing the relationship with Him was a struggle for me. Reading my Bible seemed redundant until a few years ago, when I learned that God always has something new for me. Every time I open His Word, I'm drawn into His story and what He wants to teach me about who He is. When we open His Word with a hunger to know more about who God is, not just what we can get out of it for ourselves, we can be transformed.

But the hard truth? We are sometimes too wrapped up in who *we* are to worry about who *God* is. So, here's the challenge. Let's be women who know God first. Let's learn who God is so we can then truly know who we are. And the beautiful truth? God has some really amazing things to say about who we are!

Go to the Word: *Read Exodus 33:12–23.*

The Lord said He would do what Moses asked. What had Moses asked for?

God had told Moses that He would lead the Israelites into the Promised Land, but they would be going through countries that belonged to many other people groups whom God would drive out before them. Moses was concerned about how this would go and was looking for some assurance from God that He would stay with His people.

God told Moses, "My presence will go with you, and I will give you rest" (verse 14).

Does knowing God is with you give you rest? Why, or why not?

Go to the Word: *At the end of Exodus 33, God told Moses that He would pass by him, so Moses could experience God's glory and goodness. Read Exodus 34:5–9, when God passed in front of Moses.*

Using these verses, make a list of character attributes of God.

Which character traits stand out to you the most? Why?

One character trait that stands out to me is that God is a gracious God. Scripture isn't filled with flawless role models (other than Jesus, of course!). David, Abraham, Moses, Paul, Mary Magdalene (and the list goes on!) were all complete messes at points in their lives. But through their stories of failure, we see God's grace, again and again.

The Psalms also show the constant, limitless reality of God's grace. This grace doesn't make sense to us in our normal, everyday lives. When we mess up repeatedly, the world is not so forgiving! But God's grace continues to cover us in a way our human minds can't truly understand.

Look up the word *grace* in a dictionary. What is the definition?

~ Go to the Word: *Read Psalm 103.*

In this psalm of David, we find him not asking God for things, but simply expressing the beauty of who God is. The picture of God and His character in this psalm is breathtaking! Sometimes we need to simply praise God for giving us the grace we don't deserve. Praising God helps us remember all the ways He has been faithful to us. How many times do you go to God only when you want or need something? Make a conscious effort this week to go to God to praise Him, not just to make a request.

Write down some of the verbs from Psalm 103 that tell what God does.

Too often the only prayer I express to God all day is "Please help my children behave like human beings and not wild animals." But when we attempt to wrap our minds around this grace that is offered to us—this unmerited favor poured out onto us—we are able to praise Him, whether our kids have gone wild or not.

PRAYER FOR REST

Pray your own prayer of praise to the Lord: Father, You are so good. There is so much about You that I'm learning and I have yet to learn. Continue to show me more about Your character and who You are so that I can grow to be more like You. Thank You for the grace You pour on me each and every day, when I don't deserve it.

Group Discussion

STARTER

When you want to get to know someone these days, what do you do? Talk about how you go about finding out what kind of person someone is.

REVIEW

1. Read Psalm 96:4–6. When is a time that God has faithfully proven His character in your life?

2. We learned in Psalm 29 that "the voice" is a representation of God's power, and God's power gives us strength. Discuss times when you struggle with accepting the strength of God's power and allow fear to overtake you. How does this hold you back from rest?

3. Read Psalm 71:18, focusing on the last few lines. It's our responsibility to carry on our God to the next generation,

not as a God shaped by our opinions, but as His Word says He is. What can you do as moms to carry on the truth of God and His Word to the next generation?

4. Discuss some of the character traits of God you wrote down from Exodus 34. How does this list make you want to live a life more at rest in the Lord? In what ways can you grow to be more like God?

5. How have you viewed God in your past, or how do you see Him right now? How did that change this week after looking at a few of the characteristics of God?

PRAYER FOR REST

Offer praise to God together. Let people randomly speak adjectives that describe who God is. After each adjective, the group can say together: "We praise You, Lord, for being [insert adjective here]." (For example, someone might say "compassionate." Then the group would respond, "We praise You, Lord, for being compassionate.") Close the prayer time by thanking God for His presence that gives us rest.

Room to Reflect

WHY DO I FEEL SO EMPTY?

I find myself asking this often throughout my week: *Why do I feel so empty?* The exhaustion and expectations of motherhood are demanding and relentless, and I put so much pressure on myself to be everything for everyone that I end up feeling completely drained at the end of the day.

From sunup to sundown (and many times during the night), I'm an on-duty mom. Even when my kids are at school and I switch to business mode, my mom brain still has a really hard time shutting off. This job has a tendency to overtake you. And that's not always a bad thing! Being a mom is incredibly rewarding, but it can also be incredibly overwhelming.

The overwhelming parts of motherhood can leave you feeling weary, restless, exhausted, and empty. But do they have to? What if we were able to let our heads hit the pillow at night feeling tired but not defeated? What if we could sleep in peace, knowing full well that the God of the universe is in complete control and we don't need to be? I think these truths would give us a lot of hope on our emptiest days.

This week we are going to look at four things that drain us: worry, anger, fear, and insecurity. These negative feelings are what the enemy can use to block us from rest and keep us on a never-ending cycle of hopelessness and emptiness. If we can train our hearts and minds to focus on the Lord and fight against these battles, rest will come more naturally and the empty days will shift to hope-filled ones, because we will find ourselves full of the goodness of God.

Day One
CONSIDER THE BIRDS
Matthew 6:25–34

I've never really been a lie-awake-at-night-and-worry type of person. I used to take pride in this fact, until I was hit hard with a horrible battle with postpartum anxiety that turned me into a completely different person. I share about this struggle in my book *Mom Up*:

> I was afraid to admit I was drowning. My chest was constantly tight from anxiety. I couldn't leave the house without gut-wrenching fear overtaking my body....
>
> Driving in the car, I contemplated how I might hit a telephone pole at just the right angle and break my arm so that I could go to the hospital for a few days and have a vacation from parenting. Suddenly a trip to the ER sounded like a great option for my weary heart and exhausted body....
>
> For months and months, I went to sleep with fear and woke up exhausted, with no desire to get out of bed. My mind raced with the *what ifs* and a constant reminder of my failures. *What if I can't do this mom thing? What if I can't control myself and I hurt someone I love? What if I mess up my kids too bad? What if I'm not cut out for this to begin with?*[1]

Maybe you can relate. As moms, I think at some point we all battle with a type of worry. But worry can overextend its welcome and take root in our hearts. Worry shifts our focus from God to me. And when we are so focused on self, we cannot find rest in the Lord, and we end up feeling completely empty.

Check all that apply to you:

__ **I lie awake at night worrying about things out of my control.**

__ **I spend a lot of time worrying about my marriage (or significant other).**

__ **I worry about my child(ren)'s future.**

__ **I worry that my child(ren) might get sick.**

__ **I've been told by people in my life that I worry too much.**

 Go to the Word: *Read Matthew 6:25–34.*

Worry shows up when our focus on God turns to ourselves. In these simple words in Matthew 6:25–34, Jesus is trying to put the focus back on our Father.

Jesus says to "consider the birds of the sky." What does He want us to consider about them?

Jesus asks, "Aren't you worth more than they?" Answer that question for yourself. Are you worth more to God than birds? If so, what does it say about you that the creator of the world cares for you?

Jesus used the example of worrying about what you would eat or drink or wear because that was fitting for His audience. The people He was speaking to didn't have much beyond those basic necessities, so He used those specific scenarios.

What would Jesus say to you if He were sitting in your living room and giving you this same speech today? Rewrite verse 31 in your own words to fit the common things you worry about.

Now, as we reflect on these things that consume our minds, how many of them are really worth worrying about? Maybe you are in the situation I was in and are battling with a mental illness that is taking a toll on your health. How much more do you think God cares for you? As Jesus commands, "Seek first the kingdom of God and his righteousness, and all these things [every object of your worry, doubt, battle, fear] will be provided for you" (verse 33, bracketed statement added).

PRAYER FOR REST

Write down some of your current worries. Ask God to see you through these struggles and remove the feeling of worry from you so that you can find rest in Him.

Day Two

TONGUES OF FIRE
James 3:2-12; Proverbs 26:18-19

There's something about motherhood that makes the ugliest parts of me show up. I can remain so chill when my husband leaves his socks on the floor or the waiter forgets to take the onions off my cheeseburger. But my kids can do the smallest thing, and it makes my blood boil.

Motherhood can stretch our emotions until we are stretched so thin, we have no room for grace and peace. But here's the deal—angry outbursts and righteousness don't go together, no matter who we are angry with or why.

When do you struggle the most with anger? Let's take a moment to recognize some of the things that set us off. Make a list and call them out so that you can be aware of what the warning signs are.

If you are pursuing a life that looks more like Jesus', the tongue is a great place to start. James tells us that our "human anger does not accomplish God's righteousness" (James 1:20). Then, if we jump ahead to chapter 3, he writes about the importance of controlling the tongue.

Go to the Word: Read James 3:2-12.

Jot down the three illustrations or comparisons James uses when he talks about controlling the tongue.

So, what is James telling us? What is interesting to note here is that the first two illustrations James uses are things that control something else. He shows how the tongue can either control us or we can control it. The third illustration is about something that may start out controlled and then goes wild—resulting in destruction and damage. Our tongues can either control or destroy.

How can someone's words actually affect the direction her life might take?

Has your lack of controlling your tongue ever resulted in damage or destruction? What happened? What did you learn from that?

In verse 9, James goes on to point out one of the most common hypocritical behaviors that Christ followers deal with—praising God with the same tongue that we use to tear others down. I don't know about you, but my tongue feels like a fire more than I'd like it to. I struggle to control it. I'll spout off with something fiery at one of my kids, and then I'll watch them walk off and say something awful to a sibling, and on the wildfire spreads. I used to wonder how they learned to talk to each other that way, and then I was gently reminded—they heard it from me first.

Our words have power. We never know how damaging the words we use can be, and it's so important that our goal be righteousness, not rightness. We should have one language—our church words should not be different from our mom words. Speak as if Jesus was sitting in the room, because HE IS!

What do you think? If you could see the effect of your words spreading like a stain or like flames of a fire, would you be slower to speak? Slower to get angry? I think so.

Go to the Word: *Read Proverbs 26:18-19.*

Rewrite these verses in your own words.

Do you lack the wisdom for what to say or do when you feel your tongue is on fire? Ask God for it. James tells us in 1:5, "If any of you lacks wisdom, he should ask God—who gives to all generously and ungrudgingly—and it will be given to him."

God's grace and wisdom cover our on-fire tongues and take the anger from the ugliest parts of our hearts. The hope of Jesus is enough for an angry mom who is fed up and continues to set word fires around her home.

PRAYER FOR REST

Read Galatians 5:22–23, where the fruit of the Spirit is listed. Write out this list and pray over each one of these character qualities, asking God to increase that characteristic in your life as you find rest in Him. You might want to write challenge statements for yourself for each fruit, such as: "This week, I will show patience with my children when they _____." For self-control, be sure to ask God to help you control your tongue!

Day Three
PLEASURE AND PROTECTION
Psalm 16

When I was five weeks pregnant with my third baby, I was bitten by a brown recluse spider on my rib cage in my sleep. I jumped out of bed, startled and in pain. After a few hours, the bite had swollen to the size of a softball. I could barely move and began to get very sick. Hours, days, and weeks were spent in hospitals, seeing doctor after doctor. It was too early to pick up a heartbeat in an ultrasound, so we had no idea if the baby was harmed or not. It took months before I was back to normal and could know that my baby was okay. Thankfully, the only permanent damage from the bite was a nasty scar. Nine months later, I gave birth to a beautifully healthy baby girl, who despite what we had anticipated, did not have Spider-Man abilities.

It was a terrifying situation to walk through. From one week celebrating a new pregnancy to the next being in a hospital bed, unsure what the future might look like. It was quite the roller coaster of emotions!

If anyone from the Bible knew what it was like to go through highs and lows, it was David. He faced many trials in his life and also had many incredibly wonderful experiences. (He probably even had a few health scares in his time, I would venture to guess.)

In Psalm 16, David asks for God's protection. He is hoping to find confidence and security in who God is. God is David's portion, a cup of blessing, and He holds the future. David praises and thanks God for all God has done for him and proclaims, "I will not be shaken" (verse 8).

✎ **Go to the Word:** *Read Psalm 16.*

Let's break down this psalm and see how we can relate to this as moms.

What do you learn about David and God's relationship by reading this psalm?

David is asking for God to rescue him, and he sets a foundation by declaring who God is to him. He proclaims that God is above all the places he seeks safety. When he writes "I have nothing good besides you," he is saying that God is his greatest treasure (verse 2). Other things may be good, but God is the greatest good. In verse 5, David claims God as his portion, the cup of blessing. And when David looks at a beautiful spread of wonderful things, God is the highest choice. Nothing will satisfy or sustain like the Lord (gasp, not even coffee!).

In verse 6, we see that we have a beautiful inheritance. Where David talks about boundary lines, he may be speaking figuratively or literally. Where he uses the phrase "pleasant places," in Hebrew this has a single meaning for "pleasures." It's the same word used in verse 11, where he talks about eternal pleasures. So, when we tie the two scriptures together, it seems like this is not a block of land, but a place of complete contentment with the Lord. The boundaries can create the idea that God Himself is the boundary in which our pleasure lies and everything within Him is good.

Read verses 7–8 again. David says that he has troubling thoughts in the night. What does he do about them?

In verse 9, David says three things about his heart, being, and body. What are those things?

When God is our portion, our protector, our pleasure, and our place of rest—we are full. Not full for a moment on the pleasures of this world, but complete and at rest in a way we never could imagine. God will bring us from a place of fear and desperation to a place of eternal pleasure. We will not be shaken when we are putting our hope and trust in Him!

PRAYER FOR REST

Are you facing some fear in your life that is shaking you? You too can stand like David today and say "I will not be shaken!" Place your trust in the Lord! Write down anything that might be creating fear in your life, and ask God to rescue you to a place of pleasure with Him.

Day Four

IDENTITY AND INSECURITY
2 Corinthians 12

In an effort to escape the messy house, the stacks of bills piled up on the kitchen counter, and the burden of the everyday mundane, I slipped into my car a little earlier than normal before school pickup to go for a quick drive. Just to take the long way around town and clear my head. Some days I find myself becoming so wrapped up in the tasks, the needs, or even my own lack, and it can be too much.

But even those roads I try to escape on seem to be paved with disappointment. *Your identity isn't found in your job, your role as a mom, in those bills on the counter, or even in that cold cup of coffee you forgot in the microwave*, God reminds me in my heart as I pull into the school. (And darn, forgot my coffee!) All of these places where I feel so insecure are the areas that the enemy loves to sneak in and lie to me, because why not?—I do most of the work for him anyway. But God wants to speak truth over me. And He wants to speak truth over you too.

What are some places in your life where you struggle with your own identity and insecurities?

We live in a culture that is all about personality tests. I'll admit, I'm a sucker for them too (ESFJ, Enneagram 1)! And while these things are fascinating to me, I think it's even more important to understand who God says we are first and foremost. I have this list that I look to when I start losing sight of my identity and how God sees me. It helps me to remember that before any of my titles, personalities, or flaws—I am a daughter of the King of the universe. I find rest in that, and I hope you do too.

**You are chosen. *(Ephesians 1:11)*
Your purpose is to bring praise and
glory to Christ. *(Ephesians 1:12)*
You are a new creation. *(2 Corinthians 5:17)*
You are made to live by the Word
of God. *(Matthew 4:4)*
There's no condemnation
in you. *(Romans 8:1)*
You have a mind-set of life and
peace. *(Romans 8:6)*
You are more than a
conqueror. *(Romans 8:37)*
You are a friend of Jesus. *(John 15:15)*
You are redeemed. *(Romans 3:24)*
You are no longer a slave to sin. *(Romans 6:6)*
You are an heir with Christ. *(Romans 8:17)*
You are accepted. *(Romans 15:7)*
Your body is a temple of the Holy
Spirit. *(1 Corinthians 6:19)*
You have been set free in
Christ. *(Galatians 5:1)***

**You are holy and blameless
before God.** *(Ephesians 1:4)*
**You are made alive with
Christ.** *(Ephesians 2:4–5)*
**You are seated in the heavens
with Christ.** *(Ephesians 2:6)*
**You are created to produce good
work.** *(Ephesians 2:10)*
You are a citizen of heaven. *(Philippians 3:20)*
**You are made complete in
Christ.** *(Colossians 2:9–10)*
**You are loved and
chosen.** *(1 Thessalonians 1:4)*

What stands out to you from this list? Who does God say you are?

In 2 Corinthians 12, Paul wrote about his mysterious "thorn in the flesh" and how he begged God to remove it from his life. Many scholars speculate about what this might have been, but I think it's nice that we don't know—because we can all relate to Paul; we all have some weakness or trouble that has caused us pain. My thorn has changed in different seasons of my life, but I can always come back to this and say, "Yeah, Paul, I get it."

When God didn't remove the thorn, Paul reported that this was how God responded: "My grace is sufficient for you, for my power is perfected in weakness." Paul then said, "Therefore, I will most gladly boast all the more about my weaknesses, so that Christ's power may reside in me. So I take pleasure in weaknesses, insults, hardships, persecutions, and in difficulties, for the sake of Christ. For when I am weak, then I am strong" (verses 9-10).

How is God's power shown through your difficulties?

How have these hard situations made you a better parent?

PRAYER FOR REST

Look over the list of statements about who we are in God, and choose one to focus on this week. Ask God to remind you of that statement as a way of finding security and contentment and peace in Him.

Group Discussion

STARTER

Talk about a time this past week when you felt like you were running on empty. What made you feel that way? What did you do about it?

REVIEW

1. Read Matthew 6:26-27 together. Share ways that you are putting your focus on yourself instead of on God and allowing worry to take over your life.

2. In James 3, we learned how our tongues can either control or damage. What is your tongue doing? When do you find it hardest to control your tongue?

3. What kind of fear is shaking you? How can you be like David and make God your portion, protector, pleasure, and place of rest?

4. Discuss some areas in which you battle with identity and insecurity. Now, wipe the slate clean! Speak truth over one another with truth! (Go back to the list in day four if you need help!)

5. Out of the four topics we studied this week, which is the biggest barrier that keeps you from rest? Worry, anger, fear, or insecurity? What steps can you take to find rest in the areas where you struggle?

PRAYER FOR REST

Let members of the group share favorite Bible verses of encouragement, if they have any. Pray together, asking God to help each of you to be filled by Him this week.

Room to Reflect

BEING BETTER AT BEING BUSY

In this season of my life, I am stretched between two school pickups, multiple practices each day after school, and games on the weekend—all while being a pastor's wife at our church, trying to maintain friendships, writing books, and keeping up a fun and stable home life.

It can be a bit much.

One recent morning, I ran into a friend at the Target Starbucks (where I typically run into all my friends!) before I settled in for a day of writing. We began discussing our schedules and how busy we both were, me with my four kids and her with her three. We promised to figure out a time to get together soon, then parted ways.

As I walked to my car, our conversation stuck with me. There's got to be a better way. We have to be better at being busy. Busy becomes our lifestyle; it becomes our norm. There's rarely a moment that I'm not moving while I'm at home with my family, and I even pride myself on this. *Look how great a mom I am! I do so much!* I convince myself.

But what happens when busy gets so busy that we forget how to rest?

By becoming good stewards of our time, embracing our seasons of life, learning to say no, and creating sanctuaries of refreshing rest—we can step out of the overwhelming busy and into a more peaceful, God-centered life.

STEWARDSHIP OF TIME
Mark 1:21–35; 6:30–31; Matthew 6:33

Busyness has become a status symbol in many cultures. We rush from one place to the next, and when a friend asks us how life is, we feel accomplished when we reply with "Busy!" We are only given 24 hours—1,440 minutes—in a day; how are we using them? We fill them up with endless activities, overflowing our schedules and maxing out our timetables. We believe that time management means cramming more things into an already overwhelmed schedule, just in order to make it fit. Take a few minutes to pause and think about your daily schedule and where you spend your time.

Are you maxing out your calendar? If 1 is "I have plenty of free time" and 10 is "I can't even see my calendar—there are too many things on it," what does your average month look like on this scale?

"Most of the things I spend time on bring me joy." True or false? Check near 1 for "Unless you think laundry is fun—nothing I do brings anyone joy." Check closer to 10 for "I'm loving every minute!" Where do you fall on this scale?

If you could remove one item from your schedule that might help bring you a little more peace, rest, and joy, what would it be?

If you took this thing out of your schedule, would you miss it? __ YES __ NO

Overall, how would you rate your ability to be a good steward of your time? Let's say 1 is "Terrible—I waste all kinds of time" and 10 is "Terrific—I've got a perfect plan for everything, including rest!" Where would you rate yourself on this scale?

One thing that can help us prioritize and make choices about how we use our time is to consider the eternal impact of events on our schedule. For example, taking care of your children has eternal impact, even if it sometimes feels mundane. But maybe joining one more activity just because your son wants to at the moment could hurt your family and take away from some rest and intentional time you might not be able to find otherwise. It's important as moms to be considerate and prayerful about the things we commit our time to.

Now, I'll be honest, this is a hard topic for me to teach on, because I don't have it mastered. So, I'll point you to the one person who did. Jesus was the ultimate example of spending time well. He never seemed in a hurry or too busy for anyone. He completely changed the world in the three short years of His earthly ministry, but He wasn't in a rush to get it done.

Not unlike a busy mom, Jesus was consistently inundated with needs and requests. He was constantly surrounded by people. But Jesus didn't just come to offer us rest; He also modeled how to rest. Let's take a look at one specific day in the life of Jesus and see how He reacted in the midst of busy and still found rest.

Go to the Word: Read Mark 1:21–35.

Jesus has just called His first disciples to follow Him, and they get to work right away.

List all the activities Jesus engages in at Capernaum.

Sounds like Jesus had a busy day, right? But keep reading. Here's where Jesus gets it right, and we so often get it wrong.

"Very early in the morning, while it was still dark, he got up, went out, and made his way to a deserted place; and there he was praying" (Mark 1:35). Jesus got some sleep and then woke early to spend time with the Father—setting the ultimate example for us in how we should recharge before we get up to take on the world again. We see Jesus repeat this example over and over throughout His ministry. He would disappear to go off to rest and pray. Jesus knew the importance of leading by example—not only for His disciples, but for us who follow Him today as well.

Why is rest even more important when you are very busy?

 Go to the Word: *Read Mark 6:30–31.*

If we skip ahead a few chapters to Mark 6, we see the disciples come to Jesus, apparently exhausted. They've been doing a lot, and they hadn't even had time to eat (sound familiar?). Jesus tells them, "Come away by yourselves to a remote place and rest for a while." Jesus shows His friends the importance of taking some of their precious time and spending it resting in the Lord. He teaches and demonstrates to them what a balanced life looks like, consistently leading the way to find rest with the Father.

You may not be able to go away to a remote place, but where can you go to find rest for a little while in your day?

What tools or resources could you use to make better use of the time you have each day?

◢ *Go to the Word:* *Read Matthew 6:33.*

Write out this verse that teaches a way to prioritize your time. How could you shift your day around so that the focus of your schedule would be on seeking God?

PRAYER FOR REST

Jeremiah 6:16 records the Lord trying to warn the people about an oncoming siege. The scripture says: "Stand by the roadways and look. Ask about the ancient paths, 'Which is the way to what is good?' Then take it and find rest for yourselves." Ask God this question: What is the way to what is good? Take a look at your schedule through God's eyes and see which items are not leading you on the path to good, but are just another busy item in an already crowded day. Pray for the wisdom and courage you need to find stillness in your busyness.

Day Two
EMBRACING YOUR SEASON
Ecclesiastes 3:1-8

"Motherhood never gets easier; it changes in seasons, and only gets richer as we learn to be more and more dependent on Jesus." My friend Nathalie and I wrote that sentence years ago when we both were walking through one of the most difficult and painful seasons of motherhood for us. Most days I wasn't sure I was going to make it out of that season in one piece. But every time I see that line, I'm reminded of all the seasons of life and of motherhood I've walked through.

In the book of Ecclesiastes, Solomon is writing about the mystery of life, time, and all the seasons we face. Chapter 3 reminds us of God's bigger plan in the grand scope of it all:

> There is an occasion for everything,
> and a time for every activity under
> heaven:
> a time to give birth and a time to die;
> a time to plant and a time to uproot;
> a time to kill and a time to heal;
> a time to tear down and a time to build;
> a time to weep and a time to laugh;
> a time to mourn and a time to dance;
> a time to throw stones and a time to
> gather stones;
> a time to embrace and a time to avoid
> embracing;
> a time to search and a time to count as
> lost;

a time to keep and a time to throw away;
a time to tear and a time to sew;
a time to be silent and a time to speak;
a time to love and a time to hate;
a time for war and a time for peace.
                    (verses 1–8)

We can learn from this text that there are times when it is appropriate to act in a certain way and times when it is not (dancing at a wedding is appropriate; dancing at a funeral likely isn't). The key to understanding why this simple truth is so important can be found in verse 11: "He has made everything appropriate in its time." Not in our time, but in God's time, there is an occasion for everything and a time for everything under heaven. There is a time to grieve the child you have buried or the marriage you have lost. There is a time to break off a hurtful relationship and there is a time to let new life in. There is a time to rejoice in the breakthrough of middle school awkwardness.

There is a time for everything.

What does your season look like? Look back at the verses from Ecclesiastes 3 and circle some of the things that may apply to your life now. Or add your own "a time to _____" phrases below to reflect things that you are involved in currently.

You may find yourself up to your eyeballs in diapers and spit-up. (I've been there—I had three in diapers at one time!) You may find yourself cooking dinner with a toddler at your feet. You may find yourself running constantly between the elementary school, middle school, and high school—trying to divide your time equally between your kids. You may find yourself with a desk full of financial aid and insurance paperwork and more really fun things your grown child is asking for help with. Wherever you find yourself today, there's a season for this, and you can love and embrace the season you are in. Stop wishing for the next thing to happen. Rest in the moment you are in right now.

How can you look at your season right now as a gift of God? Jot down some blessings you have experienced through this time.

As Matthew Henry says it, "To expect unchanging happiness in a changing world, must end in disappointment."[1] I can't tell you how much my happiness is measured by my disappointment in my ever-changing circumstances. But there's a time for everything, and we can set the scale to bring the expectations of the day back to reality. When you're in a season of busy, anticipate it, work with it, and flow with it. When you're in a season of pain, allow yourself to grieve, ask for help, and let others in. When you're in a season with a bit of free space, give away to those in need and open yourself up.

Examine your expectations and disappointments based on your reality. Do they make sense? What could you change?

PRAYER FOR REST

There is a time to keep and a time to throw away. Think about what appointments you need to keep this week—make sure one of those is your appointment with God. Ask God to show you what you might need to throw away in order to keep spending more time with Him.

Day Three
THE POWER OF OUR YES AND NO
1 Chronicles 14:8–10

Come in close; I need to share a secret. I have a problem. A real problem. Are you ready?

I struggle with saying no.

"Can you serve on the PTA?" *You bet I can!* "Would you make cookies for the bake sale?" *Are eight dozen enough?* "Can you serve on this committee, lead that Bible study, and drive this carpool?" *Sure, okay, and why not?*

Saying no and creating boundaries can be hard. Maybe you're good at this, but I haven't always been. Over the past couple of years, my schedule was more full than usual, so I knew I had to practice saying no. It wasn't easy, and I didn't always do a good job. I committed to some things that I wish I had said no to, but I was grateful I did say no to the things I did (after I let the guilt slip away!). As busy women and moms, we simply can't and shouldn't do it all. It's not healthy or wise.

Do you struggle with saying yes to too many things? Make a list of things that you could say no to in this season of life that might help bring a little more rest to your life.

King David was well known for being a man after God's own heart. As the king, it was really important for him to follow the instruction from the Lord and know when to say yes and when to say no in certain circumstances. Now, I know what you're thinking, what does your saying no to help with the bake sale have to do with running a kingdom? But don't you think God considers the work that you're doing running your household as important as the work of David running the kingdom? I think so!

Go to the Word: *Read 1 Chronicles 14:8–10.*

In 1 Chronicles 14, we find King David establishing his house and rule over Israel. David's success also brought challenges from the outside, and the Philistines were a constant enemy of whoever was on the throne in Israel. In verse 9, the Philistines have raided the Valley of Rephaim, which lies southwest of Jerusalem, between Judah and Benjamin (Joshua 15:8). So, it seems like a no-brainer to fight back against the Philistines.

But instead of heading off into battle, David goes to God *first* with a question: "Should I attack them? Yes or no?" He doesn't rush into anything. He wants to know whether God will be on his side or not. Because David knows the truth—if God tells him to fight, then God Himself will be with him in the battle. God does say yes, and He leads David and the Israelites to win the battle against the Philistines.

How might David's story have looked different if he had run into battle without seeking the Lord? What does this look like in your own life when you don't allow God to help guide your steps and decisions?

Saying yes isn't always a bad thing. God has glorious things for us in this life that He wants us to take in and enjoy, and maybe sometimes a battle or two He may want to fight with us.

There is power in our yeses and in our noes; the secret is to let God into the decision-making process. Instead of spouting off yes or even no to every opportunity presented, pause. Step back and take some time to prayerfully consider what God might have for you in those opportunities.

What opportunities are you trying to decide about right now? Write down those potential decisions. Consider the schedule you have now and the schedule you will have if you take more things on. Will you still have opportunities to find rest in the Lord? Who in your life will be impacted by your yes or no?

PRAYER FOR REST

Look over your list of potential decisions and ask God to help you with each one.

Day Four

THE SANCTUARY OF HOME
Acts 28:16–31; 3 John 1:5–8

There's something about a full, busy schedule that makes me crave the comfort of home. This past year we were as intentional as we could be to make sure we had at least one evening when all of us were home with no activities after school, and it was glorious (for the most part). The busyness of life makes me ache for time to spend lying on the couch reading books with my kids, sitting down together as a family to eat dinner, or just simply being *home*.

I've always looked at our home as a sanctuary. A place where we feel safe, loved, and rested. I work hard to keep it as clean as possible—with four kids and a chocolate lab, it's far from perfect, but so are we. If we can come back from a day of work and school and find peace and rest in our sanctuary of home, then I feel like I am doing something good for my family.

What does the atmosphere of your home feel like? Rank how close or far you feel from having a sanctuary.

Out of control   Sanctuary of rest

Our homes can also be a place of rest and renewal for others. The apostle Paul shows us this in Acts 28. While he was traveling in Rome, he felt at home and decided to stay. Verses 30–31 tell us, "Paul stayed two whole years in his own rented house. And he welcomed all who visited him, proclaiming the kingdom of God and teaching about the Lord Jesus Christ with all boldness and without hindrance."

Paul set the example that hospitality isn't about having a perfect house—we can invite others in and share Jesus with them regardless of where we live and what it looks like.

Look up some definitions for *hospitality* and write them below:

I used to think my house had to be huge and perfectly put together to be a place to welcome others in. But after years in ministry, I've learned that it's not about that at all. My kids don't care about the size of our house; they care about the love and joy that are found there. Our visitors don't care about spotless floors or my slightly outdated kitchen. They know we make good burgers and provide a safe space for love and compassion.

Go to the Word: Read 3 John 1:5-8.

Hospitality was important in biblical times because there were no hotels, and traveling people often had to rely on the hospitality of strangers or family members in order to have a place to stay. Why do you think it's still important to open up your home?

Years ago, I had the opportunity to take a trip to Israel, and there, I learned a lot about the culture during the time of Jesus' earthly ministry. Hospitality was everything. They didn't have soccer practices or phones to distract them. When a person came into another's home, it was a place of rest and peace.

One evening on our trip, we got to partake in an authentic dinner from biblical times. The scene was set for us to experience what an evening might have been like for the people we read about in Scripture. We entered the home and sat on pillows and rugs scattered around a low table. Dinner lasted for hours. No one looked at a phone or had to run out to something else. We just sat, rested, and enjoyed the presence of one another.

This is rest. This is home. This is sanctuary.

When I got home, part of me wanted to throw away my dining room chairs and cut the legs off my tables and make a total lifestyle change. While it didn't take long for us to get back into the busyness of our lives, those slow evenings in Israel are a wonderful memory that we carry with us as a reminder of the sanctuary of home.

Psalm 127:1 says, "Unless the LORD builds a house, its builders labor over it in vain." How have you made your home a refuge of rest for your family and others? What can you do to allow the Lord to build up your household and find space for more rest and peace in the midst of your busy life?

PRAYER FOR REST

Write out a prayer and ask God to use your home to bless your family and bring rest and peace to those who enter its walls.

WEEK FOUR

Group Discussion

STARTER

Just for fun, pull out your calendars or just talk about what is in your schedule on a weekly basis.

REVIEW

1. The things you spend your time on have eternal impact. How can you make the best use of the time you have?

2. Seasons in motherhood are constantly changing. What does your season look like, and how is God using this season to work in you? How do you need to shift your expectations and attitude to match the season you're in?

3. In 1 Chronicles 14:8–10, we learn that David went to God first before heading straight into battle. What does this teach us about how we should respond to all

circumstances? Are there things in your life you need to approach God about before saying yes or no to them?

4. In Acts 28, Paul sets the example that a home can be a refuge of rest, a sanctuary of peace. What is the atmosphere of your home? What needs to change in your home to create more rest? Encourage others in ways that help you all to find peace in the sanctuary of home.

5. Discuss ways that you can make some changes in your schedule to find more stillness and peace and say no to some of the busyness. Make a commitment to challenge one another to be better at being busy.

PRAYER FOR REST

Draw a simple house shape on a piece of paper. Let each group member write a word (or words) inside the house that represents a way to make the home a sanctuary of rest. Pray together, asking God to help you find the ability to offer hospitality well—to your own family members and to others who may come across your paths.

Room to Reflect

GRACE

Grace is such a basic biblical principle and yet such a hard idea to fully wrap our minds around. Mercy and grace are often mistaken one for the other. Mercy is defined as *not* getting what we do deserve. Grace is defined as being freely given what we *don't* deserve.

We show our children grace when we care for them, no matter what their behavior is at the time. My daughter may slam a door in my face out of anger, but I will still feed her lunch that day. She may lose her jacket at school, but I'll still clothe her. We do these things because we love our children, not because they have done anything to deserve it. And in fact, they may deserve to go to bed without dinner or to be made to wear last year's clothes, but often, instead of punishing them for every careless or disobedient act, we offer grace.

The same goes for us and the grace of God. We are dirty, rotten sinners, but regardless, we are shown grace through faith, as a gift from God, not through works (Ephesians 2:8–9)! There is nothing we can do to earn merit with the Lord. We are His children through faith, and that is enough!

Day One
WEAKNESS
2 Corinthians 12:8–10; Judges 7:1–11; Luke 7:36–50

Have you ever seen the show *American Gladiators*? It's a lot like professional wrestling mixed with an obstacle course. The show had over a dozen "gladiators" who were billed as the biggest, toughest all-around athletes. There were male and female gladiators, from various backgrounds and experiences, but they all had one thing in common: these people were incredibly strong and had crazy endurance.

Were all the contestants great at the challenges? No way, and that's what made the show entertaining.

Weakness is not a trait that is admired in our culture. Actually, I don't know that there is any culture that admires weakness. People don't want to be seen as weak—not just weak physically, but emotional, intellectual, and even relational weaknesses are treated as things to be removed quickly from a person's life by any means necessary.

However, God does not see the world the way we do. And in His eyes, the weak can be strong. In this study, we'll look at some weaklings to see how God uses the weak to reveal the strength of His grace.

Go to the Word: *Read 2 Corinthians 12:8–10.*

In your own words, what does the Lord tell Paul in verse 9? What does that mean to you?

Read on into verse 10. Why does Paul say he will boast about his weaknesses?

Go to the Word: Read Judges 7:1–11.

In Judges 6, an angel comes to Gideon and tells him that he will be the warrior to deliver Israel out of the hands of the Midianites. But this comes as a big surprise to Gideon, who says he is from the family that is "the weakest in Manasseh" and that he is the youngest (6:15). Nevertheless, God chooses Gideon to be the one to lead the battle. In Judges 7, God takes His support of weakness one step further by whittling down Gideon's available fighters.

In Judges 7:2, what reason does the Lord give for saying that Gideon has too many troops?

God is not without compassion toward us humans, who often don't understand His plans. In 7:9–11, God realizes that leaving Gideon with only three hundred men may have the poor boy feeling nervous. What encouragement does He offer Gideon?

In this story of Gideon, he did not deserve to be the general of the armies of Israel, but that is exactly what he became. Just like Gideon, we do not deserve to be the servant of God or a follower of Jesus. However, what we receive from Jesus is far greater than anything we could ever muster on our own. This is grace in practice. We do not deserve to be used by Him, and yet He strengthens and equips us and encourages us in His service.

 Go to the Word: *Read Luke 7:36-50.*

In this story, Simon the Pharisee was hosting a gathering at his home and had invited Jesus—not because he wanted to follow Jesus, but probably out of curiosity, or to increase the number of guests coming to his party (since Jesus had already become known by then). The Pharisees were a powerful bunch, and since Simon was hosting people, it's safe to assume he was living comfortably.

How is the woman described who comes to the Pharisee's house?

Women in this culture were already considered weak, but this particular woman had a bad reputation and would have fallen into the lower rungs of society. But she brought an expensive jar of perfume and used it on Jesus, anointing His feet as if they were the feet of a king, instead of just the dusty feet of a traveling teacher from Nazareth.

Simon questioned why Jesus, if He were really a prophet, would allow this unclean sinner to touch Him. To answer Simon, Jesus told a story about two debtors. Both debtors were forgiven their debts, but one owed ten times more than the other.

How did Jesus compare the debtors with the woman who washed His feet?

Jesus elevated this woman from her low position by respecting her humble act of worship and forgiving her sins before everyone in the Pharisee's house.

What did Jesus tell the woman in verse 50?

We can rest in the peace the Lord gives us through His grace. We can boast in the Lord because His strength is ours. That is the grace we receive: His strength and peace that come through the gift of forgiveness.

Perhaps the Lord is calling you to do something that you are not comfortable doing. This may be an opportunity for the Lord to use you in a way beyond your own strength to accomplish His goals. Through your weakness, He will be given the glory and, so, draw more people to Him.

If the Lord can use the weakness of Paul, the smallness of Gideon's army, and the humility of a sinner's offering, He can most assuredly use you!

Does feeling or appearing weak scare you? Why, or why not?

PRAYER FOR REST

Repeat the words of Paul from 2 Corinthians 12:10, "When I am weak, then I am strong." Offer your weakness up to God today and ask for His gracious strength.

Day Two

GRACE AND LAW

Galatians 3:10-14; Deuteronomy 27-28; Romans 3:10-24

"Mommy, look at me! Look what I can do!" My girls love to have my full and undivided attention, as I'm sure your children do as well. They love to perform their own rendition of *The Nutcracker* or recite their Girl Scout oath flawlessly, waiting with bated breath for the inevitable praise and adoration they know I'll have for them. If I look away for even a moment, they have to start all over again.

Even from a young age, a temptation of humans is to *do* in order to be noticed, respected, or loved. We learn this trait from infancy; it's embedded in our very nature. If we can only perform well enough, test high enough, or please enough people, we will be seen as *good*. However, we are told from Scripture that in reality no one is righteous, not even one.

Following the law or doing works is not enough to overcome our rebellion against God. Our limited good cannot undo the wrong we have done.

Go to the Word: Galatians 3:10-14.

Reading verse 10, what does Paul write concerning those who rely on works of the Law?

✍ **Go to the Word:** *Read Deuteronomy 27:9–26; 28:1–14.*

The last half of Galatians 3:10 is a quotation from Deuteronomy
27:26. Deuteronomy 27 and 28 outline blessings and curses for
Israel. These are the rewards for following the Law and conse-
quences for breaking the Law. In the space provided, list some
of these blessings and curses. (You don't have to write them
all, just a few of each will do.)

Blessings

Curses

**Galatians 3:11 states that no one is _____
before God by the Law.**

There is no other way for our sin to be dealt with unless
it is paid for. The curse of the Law must be satisfied. Verse 13
explains how Jesus became our curse.

**Think about that for a moment. How does this impact
your thoughts and feelings about the crucifixion?**

✍ **Go to the Word:** *Read Romans 3:10–24.*

Romans 3 sounds a lot like Galatians 3. In Romans 3:21–22, Paul brings up the idea of being declared righteous. This is the definition of justification. Because Jesus died the appropriate death, a death that dealt with the curse of sin and the curse of the Law, we have the possibility of being declared righteous before the Father. This righteousness would not be our own righteousness—able to be achieved through our own means.

According to Romans 3:22, how do we get the righteousness of God?

Jesus displays His righteousness by fulfilling the Law (Matthew 5:17) and not abolishing it. The requirements are completed; the contract is fulfilled. This paved the way for the new covenant in His blood, which was first celebrated at the Last Supper (Matthew 26:28; Luke 22:20).

Righteousness can also refer to a right relationship between two parties. We practice this in our own families, to a degree. We would never treat our great-grandmother in the same way we would treat our younger sister. There is a kind of right relationship that is expected.

God expects us to interact with Him in a specific manner, and Jesus refers to this concept in a sermon to His disciples (Matthew 5–7; Luke 6:20–49). Jesus states in Matthew 7:21 that not everyone who cries out "Lord!" to Him will be allowed to enter the kingdom of heaven. He is looking for those who do the will of the Father, who display true righteousness. And the righteousness Jesus is looking for only comes through a right relationship with Him, through faith in Him.

Grace is a gift given because of the work Jesus did, not a wage earned by accomplishing a certain list of tasks. By focusing on our own works and how they measure up, we miss out on the relationship we can have with the Father through Jesus.

Rewrite Galatians 3:24 in your own words.

PRAYER FOR REST

It can be hard for us to let go of the idea that we have to do more, do better, do everything we can in order to be justified before God. But that work has already been done for us. Ask God to help you let go of the idea that good works are required—either to receive God's grace or to be considered a "good enough" Christian. Ask to receive the rest that comes in knowing Jesus has paid the price for our sins.

Day Three

GIFTS OF GRACE

Ephesians 4:7–15; 1 Corinthians 12:4–11; 1 Peter 4:10–11

Recently we were looking back on some little photo albums—just searching for a funny photo to show the kids. Of course, we can never find just the photo we want, so we ended up looking through quite a few. It's fun to see the girls grow up, and especially fun to see them grow up together. What's particularly funny is to hear our second and third daughters ask where they are in some of the pictures.

"Oh, you weren't born yet" is an odd concept to really grasp when you are young.

"Was I in your tummy then, Mama?"

"Nope, that was a few years before you were born," I'll answer.

The culture of our family has shifted as more kids have entered the picture. With one baby, bath time was an event. With four kids, it's a process that has to be scheduled. In some families with only one child, time with parents doesn't have to be shared. For families with many children, time with parents is a limited resource that must be shared. And there is not a bottomless pit of energy to draw from.

The concept of sharing takes some time for children to understand. For some of us adults, having kids has shown us how much we still need to learn about sharing.

Our Father in heaven also has some things to teach us about sharing. He expects us to share what He gives us.

Go to the Word: Read Ephesians 4:7–15.

What three things does verse 8 say that Christ did?

Let's take a look at these. First, Christ "ascended on high." Why is that significant? It's important to note because it describes our Savior's position. He ascended and is seated at the right hand of the Father, and as He stated in Matthew 28, He has been given all authority. And in that authority, He has given gifts to the people.

In verse 11, what five groups received "gifts" from Christ?

And what are these five groups of people supposed to do according to verse 12?

You may be thinking that you don't fall into any of those categories, but think again. If you care for people, you are a kind of pastor. If you have ever explained anything about the

Bible or Jesus to someone, you are a teacher (you don't need a certificate for this kind of teaching). We are all part of the body of Christ, and it is the responsibility of all of us to "reach unity in the faith and in the knowledge of God's Son" (verse 13).

How do we do this? Thankfully, not on our own.

When we follow Jesus, He sends the Holy Spirit to reside in every believer. From the Spirit, every believer receives at least one gift, and this gift is given to use in the life of a child of God. We are not just left to our own willpower and ingenuity. We have been equipped for the work of ministry.

Go to the Word: Read 1 Corinthians 12:4–11.

What are the different gifts listed in these verses that are given by the Spirit? List a few below.

Go to the Word: Read 1 Peter 4:10–11.

What do these verses state we should do with the gifts that we are given from the Spirit?

They are called spiritual *gifts*—we did not earn these abilities or attributes. God gave these gifts to us to use to minister to the body of Christ. We are supposed to be "dispensers" of the grace that we receive from our God.

This is really the next level of understanding grace. Why do we receive from the Lord? So we can give back to others. We give as we have been given. Grace was freely given to us; part of our responsibility now is to give it out to others. That's how the ministry of grace works.

PRAYER FOR REST

Thank God for the gifts He has given us, and if you are unsure, ask Him to make it clear to you what gifts you have been given so far through the Spirit.

Day Four

SHARING GRACE WITH THOSE WHO NEED IT MOST

Matthew 5:43–48; Romans 5:6-10

High school reunion. How do those words make you feel? For some, this American cultural phenomenon creates a sense of awkward terror. That's right; some of us are just old enough to institutionally be pressured to go back again.

Now, not everyone had a terrible time in high school; some have great memories, probably from extracurricular activities or because of that one best friend. For many, though, there are memories of being bullied or feeling inadequate. We get past those things as adults, but all it takes sometimes is seeing the name of that one mean girl, and we shrink back into our sixteen-year-old cocoon of a woman.

A high school reunion may bring us face to face with this foe we have tried to forget. Maybe some of you even were someone's enemy. In that case, you may have other emotions to deal with, such as shame or guilt.

Jesus and His disciples also had enemies. However, these enemies did more than write gossip on the bathroom wall with a Sharpie. The first-century bullies used threats of injury, pain, prison, or even death. The system the Romans had placed over the Jews (and used at times to the advantage of the Jewish leaders) was oppressive and intimidating. The Romans were a constant enemy presence in the Jewish homeland. There was no outgrowing this enemy.

Go to the Word: *Read Matthew 5:43-48.*

Fill in the blank from verse 43: "You have heard that it was said, _____ and

_____."

This sounds good. This sounds like what the Lord would have for us, right? Loving neighbors is good. And hating enemies? Well, that seems natural. However, if we read on in verses 44–45, we get an even greater teaching from Jesus.

Fill in the blank: "But I tell you, _____

_____ and _____

_____, so that you may be children of your Father in heaven."

Jesus is calling His disciples to a greater righteousness. He is calling all those who follow Him to do the harder thing. He calls those who are His followers to love their enemies, even to the point of praying for the ones who bring pain into their lives through persecution.

Honestly, this sounds close to impossible. Think about that bully in high school. Some of us still haven't really forgiven her. Jesus wants us not just to forgive that person, but to love her.

So, the big question is, how are we supposed to do this? Do we bake her a cake? Well, maybe.

The answer is *grace*. We offer the person grace. We speak grace to her, we act graciously toward her, and we refrain from returning evil back to her. If we remember our definition of *grace*, it is receiving something that is not deserved. Truly an enemy does not deserve kindness from us.

Go to the Word: *Read Romans 5:6–10.*

From the context of this passage, who are the ungodly identified in verse 6?

Verse 7 reveals how difficult this concept is for us. What will someone rarely do according to this verse?

How did God prove His love for us (verse 8)?

Have you thought about that fact lately? We were the enemies of God. We rebelled against Him; we disrespected Him. And yet, while we were still in that category, Jesus gave His life for us, His enemies. This truth, even as I type it, hits my heart hard. What love He shows to us! What an amazing Savior! And what a good Master, that He calls us to follow His example. We are to love as Jesus does. Grace has been given to us so we can be the ones to give it to others. Our enemies need the life-changing power of the gospel. Who else needs it more?

And what better way to love our enemies than to give them the gift of Christ?

Who in your life right now would you place, even loosely, in the category of "enemy"?

What are some practical ways to love someone who does not love you back?

PRAYER FOR REST

One way we can enter into rest in the Lord is through our right relationship with God. But another powerful way to obtain the peace of mind and heart that comes in the Lord's rest is to build right relationships with everyone in our lives—including and perhaps especially with our enemies. Ask God to help you take steps toward repairing any relationships in your life that need to be made right.

Group Discussion

STARTER

Tell about a time when you deserved punishment, but instead a parent or other authority figure offered you grace. How did you feel about that?

REVIEW

1. Why do you think weakness is seen as such a bad thing in our culture? Discuss your personal experiences within your group.

2. Are there ways in which you still rely on works as a means to your salvation? We need to be aware of things that we try to do to appease God or our own guilty conscience. Talk about what you do, even in your own mind, to try to be worthy of God's grace.

3. How does the idea that we can't simply do better to undo the wrong we have done make you feel? Is it a relief? Does it worry you? Explain your response.

4. What spiritual gifts do you think the Lord has given you? How have you been encouraged to use your gifts?

5. How can we become better at loving our enemies? What would that look like for you?

PRAYER FOR REST

Encourage group members to think about someone to whom they need to offer grace and to show love in Jesus' name—whether that person is an enemy or not. If you want, invite everyone to give the first initial of the person they are thinking about. Then form a circle and ask God to give you rest through repairing broken relationships or reaching out to those who don't deserve God's gift of grace (just like us). Pray for the person on your right, lifting up the initial of the unnamed person.

Room to Reflect

PSALM 23

"The Lord is my Shepherd, I shall not want ..." If you grew up going to church, you most likely heard or even prayed Psalm 23 many times. I know for myself, as a child, it became simply words on a page. I was expected to memorize it in exchange for candy or a small toy, but I heard it so often that the meaning sort of fell away. Even unbelievers hear it and are comforted.

Just because Psalm 23 is familiar, though, doesn't mean we fully grasp what it says. In this week, we are going to dive deeper into the famous psalm. Even if you think you have all the understanding this chapter of Scripture has to offer, I challenge you to dig down and find unexpected treasure that the Lord has planted here for our benefit.

Day One

THE LORD IS MY SHEPHERD
Isaiah 53:6; Luke 15:3–7; Psalm 23:1–2

My children, like most, are obsessed with animals. *All* animals! We live near a lot of farmland, and whenever we pass a field with sheep or horses, they go crazy! "Look at the sheeeeeeeep! They are sooooo cuuuuute!" Though they are cute, sheep are funny creatures. They are livestock—animals people raise for food or other uses. Sheep provide wool, which is amazing! But what also makes them unique is how helpless they really are. Sheep are very ill equipped to protect themselves. They are in constant need of care and protection. They are in need of provision from the shepherd.

Go to the Word: *Read Isaiah 53:6.*

What does the Bible say about sheep and people?

Go to the Word: *Read Luke 15:3–7.*

Let's look at this parable that Jesus taught to His disciples concerning the character and reputation of this good shepherd.

What is the dilemma the shepherd is faced with?

Losing one sheep out of a hundred amounts to a 1 percent loss. Would everyone respond to this problem the way the shepherd in the story does? Why, or why not?

What is the (slightly odd) response of the shepherd when he returns with the lost sheep?

What do you think? If you found a lost possession or even a pet, would you have a party and invite the neighbors? This shepherd is all about his sheep. He clearly loves them. And this love extends beyond what the sheep can ever deliver back to him. This is in keeping with the description we receive about the shepherd in Psalm 23, who is identified as the Lord.

Go to the Word: Read Psalm 23:1–2.

The first verse is a summary of the entire psalm. David is writing this psalm and shares the fact that Yahweh is his shepherd. Many Bible translations show the word for "Lord" in the Old Testament set off in all caps. When the word *Lord* is printed in all capital letters, this signifies that the word is actually *YHWH* (often shown as Yahweh). This is the covenant name of God that identifies Him.

The shepherd being talked about in this psalm can be none other than the God of Abraham, Isaac, and Jacob. And comparing God to a shepherd would have been a familiar word picture at the time—a way of helping hearers of the psalm relate to who God is to them.

Where does the shepherd lead the sheep in verse 2, and why are those places significant?

The good shepherd in this psalm leads his sheep not only to a pleasant place, but he also leads them to the things that are necessary to life. Cool water and lush pasture are what a sheep needs. The sheep have grass to eat, water to drink, pasture to rest in, and the protection of their shepherd. They are cared for and without worry. This is such a beautiful picture of what God does for us.

Do you struggle with worrying about having everything you need? The Lord offers us simplicity in His provision. If we, like trusting sheep, trust our Good Shepherd, we will not be lacking for anything. We will have everything we need.

What are our challenges to trusting our Shepherd to provide for us? What is it that keeps us from contentment?

When we think of what it means to lack nothing, how would we describe this related to our own situation?

How would our Good Shepherd, Jesus, describe lacking nothing? What are some of His promises to provide for us?

PRAYER FOR REST

Praise the Lord, your Good Shepherd, for providing what you need today. Trust Him and rest in that trust.

Day Two

HE RENEWS AND LEADS ME

John 10:27–28; Psalm 23:3–4; Deuteronomy 9:25–29

My third daughter has some serious gumption. She will march right up to her older sisters and boss them around like it's her job. Just the other day, she asked to play in her room, but we told her she needed to wait until the baby woke up. In response, she sneaked into her room and flipped on the lights.

"Oh, look! The baby is awake!"

Of course, a conversation about selfishness and thinking of others as more important than ourselves ensued, and I could see her four-year-old mind trying to understand why she couldn't just have what she wanted the moment she wanted it. The idea of being selfless still didn't make logical sense. Why wouldn't she just try really hard or do anything she could to get what she really wanted?

Humility as a virtue is not natural. It must be modeled and considered and taught. Being a follower requires humility. But for humans, our default mode is pride and selfishness.

Some of us often have difficulty following someone else's direction. We are definitely not helped to acknowledge this in the American culture of independence. Our self-centeredness can lead us to strike out on our own, even to our own detriment. There is an old saying: a smart person learns from their mistakes, but a wise person learns from someone else's mistakes. Following and learning from others can help us through trying times. Someone who has gone on before can help us to learn lessons long before we are confronted with the same situation.

Think of someone who has spoken wisdom into your life and taught you some life lessons. What did that person teach you?

Take a few minutes to reach out and thank that person today.

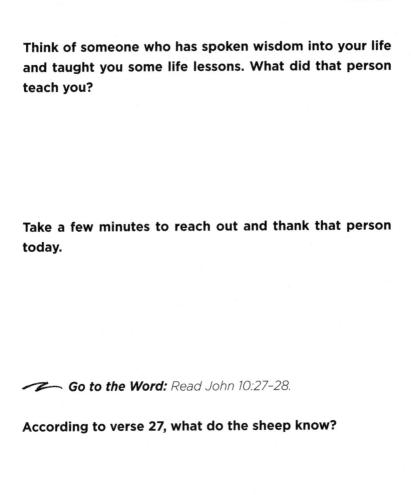 **Go to the Word:** *Read John 10:27-28.*

According to verse 27, what do the sheep know?

What do the "sheep" receive from Jesus?

Jesus speaks to His sheep—His people. He calls to them. If a person with faith hears Jesus, that person will follow Him.

For those of us who are a little more cautious about sharing our faith in Jesus, this should be incredibly encouraging. If we share the gospel, and the people we speak to are ready to be His followers, then they will respond like sheep hearing their shepherd's voice. We don't have to be the most eloquent preacher or the most powerful evangelist. Jesus has called each one of us to Christ, but the work of faith in someone's heart, that is firmly in the Lord's hands.

Acknowledging that we need help can be a true struggle. There is a sense of accomplishment to be able to say, "I did it!" But the truth is, we know that we are needy creatures. We need companionship and encouragement. We need advice and accountability. Not only are we limited people who need help from others, but we are in need of renewal. Even the things that we can accomplish ourselves eventually tire us. We are not unlimited and omnipotent beings. The Lord knows this. This is why He established a pattern of rest after work has been accomplished.

Go to the Word: *Read Psalm 23:3.*

In the space provided, rewrite the verse.

The Good Shepherd restores the sheep. He not only knows what they need to live, but He knows what they need to keep on going. The role that the shepherd plays in the life of the sheep is that of sustainer. But why? Why would a shepherd put forth so much effort for such needy creatures? Verse 3 offers one reason. It states that the shepherd leads his sheep correctly for the sake of his reputation. Some translations say "for his name's sake." This concept is important.

In Deuteronomy 9, God becomes extremely angry with the nation of Israel. Actually, that is an understatement. Yahweh has become enraged at their rebellious attitude and general ungratefulness. He states that He would rather destroy all of them and start over with Moses and make a nation from him. Moses prays before the Lord.

✍ **Go to the Word:** *Read Deuteronomy 9:25–29.*

What is the reason that Moses gives to the Lord to not destroy His people?

Essentially, Moses is calling God's bluff in this passage. He has already made so many promises to other people in generations past, like Abraham, Isaac, Jacob, Joseph, and basically all the original heads of the tribes of Israel. Not only this, but God made His intentions clear to all Egypt and the other tribes and peoples that they wandered past in the wilderness. If the Lord abandoned Israel now, what would the world think when they encountered the name of Yahweh?

They would think that God was unable to accomplish His promises, that He was weak, or that He was a liar. None of those things is true, but that would be God's reputation among the nations. The Lord acts in a way consistent with His own character and reputation. Yahweh will be faithful to His Word and to His name.

 Go to the Word: *Read Psalm 23:4.*

According to this verse, where does God sometimes lead His sheep?

What is the reaction of the sheep to this leading, and why?

Because the Lord is consistent and because He has shown Himself to be good and trustworthy, even if the path the shepherd leads the sheep on seems treacherous, the sheep stay with Him. They know He will act according to His character. The sheep trust the shepherd. They trust Him in pleasant meadows, and they trust Him through dark valleys. They know that He is able to protect and comfort them. Do we trust our Shepherd like that? Do you trust your Shepherd like that?

PRAYER FOR REST

Use verses 3 and 4 of Psalm 23 to guide your prayer. Thank God for renewing your life and for leading you on right paths. Thank Him for the comfort He provides in dark times.

Day Three
HE REFRESHES AND ANOINTS ME
Psalm 23:5; Luke 16:19–31

"Mom, are we there yet?!" How many times have you heard this phrase yelled at you from the back seat of your minivan? Road trips with kids are both fun and horrific at the same time. Everyone needs something—a game to play, a snack, a potty break. You spend half the trip stopping along the way for refreshment in some form or another. But what everyone is waiting for is to finally be there. We are looking for the final refreshment of that hotel room or rental home, where we can finally kick off our shoes, shower, or go for a swim.

It's easy for us to get wrapped up in big-picture ideas about God; that He is to be feared, that He is all powerful, and so on. But we forget sometimes that He is a God who wants to know and understand us. He wants to provide for our needs and even some of our wants. He desires pleasure and refreshment for us.

Go to the Word: *Read Psalm 23:5.*

This verse marks a shift in the psalm. Instead of sheep and shepherds, the language shifts to talking about a kind of banquet. When David was writing this psalm, he had possibly been working in Saul's court as a musician. Perhaps this is what David had in mind—one of the royal banquets. What is interesting is the context of this banquet.

Where is the prepared table situated?

Think about this scene—his enemy is close enough to observe him, and yet instead of running away or preparing to fight, David is at such ease in the presence of God, he is content to sit and have a banquet in plain sight. Perhaps even sitting at the same table as those who might plot against him.

He has no reason to fear, because he is sitting under the protection and power of the host—a host who is confident about maintaining the peace.

What does David say happens at the table?

The second half of Psalm 23:5 talks about being anointed with oil. Anointing people with oil for good health or as part of daily hygiene was a common practice of the time. But anointing with oil was also done in ceremonies to show favor being given to a special person for an important post—such as anointing a king. Here, it appears that the psalm writer is praising God for providing special care in every way. The table is prepared. His head is anointed with perfumed oil. His cup is filled to overflowing. He is satisfied in every way, and then some. He is an honored guest, and is grateful for the honor.

What does this description of the psalmist at the table tell you about God?

↗ **Go to the Word:** *Read Luke 16:19–31.*

What is the name of the poor beggar in this passage?

In verse 23, who was next to Abraham?

Who called Abraham "Father" in verse 24?

The Lord often gives the preferred place to those who are without honor in our world. God's perspective is different from ours. In this story, the rich man, who probably had banquets often, would have missed out on the eternal banquet that the Lord prepared for those whom He wished to honor.

David was the youngest in a family of brothers. No one regarded him as great or worthy of honor, and yet it was the Lord who saw him and lifted him up to be the anointed king of Israel.

The Lord has given us honor as His children through the Son. Because of who Jesus is and His character, He notices those who are often overlooked. He lifts the head of the humble (Psalm 3:3).

PRAYER FOR REST

The Lord is for us, He cares for us, and He honors us. Use Psalm 91 as your prayer today and as a way of entering into rest with the Lord.

Day Four

HE PURSUES ME

Psalm 23:6; 1 Samuel 23:24–28

Have you ever watched a predator stalk its prey? Cats patiently follow squirrels. They move slowly and then stop. All the while, they continue to focus on the prey, measuring their steps, calculating how many leaps it might take to pounce upon it. When the squirrel looks away, the cat moves forward quickly, getting closer. When the cat is close enough, it strikes! It moves quickly to surprise the squirrel. The squirrel may try to run, but the cat runs faster. The predator swipes at the squirrel to snag it, but then it can't stop in time and scrambles over the fuzzy creature, flipping on top of it.

In Psalm 23, we read that goodness and mercy will be in pursuit of the writer all the days of his life. The word here for "pursue" is the same as what is used to describe a predator stalking its prey. Normally we think of a predator hunting prey as a negative thing for the prey—doom is just around the corner. But this act is just a natural part of animal life. It's an intense moment because there is pressure on the predator to make the kill. No kill, no food; that's just the way things go. If the predator has cubs at home in the den, there will be no food for them either.

⟞ **Go to the Word:** *Read Psalm 23:6.*

How is the word picture presented in this verse a shift from the rest of the psalm in some ways?

The first five verses of Psalm 23 are all from the sheep's per-spective and create a peaceful, comforting image. But the idea of something in pursuit of someone stirs up images of wolves stalking sheep at night.

However, the predator in this imagery is not a hungry wolf. It is God's goodness and mercy, or faithful love. Some of the best examples of God's goodness pursuing David are during a period when David was being pursued by a different predator, namely King Saul.

Go to the Word: *Read 1 Samuel 23:24–28.*

In reading verse 26, who had the upper hand in this situation?

In verses 27 and 28, what did the Lord use to deliver David out of the hands of King Saul?

The intensity with which Saul hunted David sounds like flat-out obsession. For the better part of ten years, Saul pursued David, and every time Saul got close, the Lord delivered David. At a certain point, you begin to lose faith in the coincidence explanation for events and instead see them for what they really are: the Lord and His goodness protecting His servant David.

When in your life have you felt the Lord pursuing you? Do you believe the Lord has your best interests in mind at all times? Why, or why not?

Some struggle with the concepts of grace and mercy. When people have wrongdoing in their past, it's hard for them to believe that God truly wants to shower them with good things. Sometimes we just have a hard time seeing how God's goodness is present in very difficult situations.

The truth is that Jesus wants to show just how good His promises are. There are times He may allow difficulty to refine us or to give us opportunity to trust Him. But His intentions for His followers are always good, and His promises can be trusted. One of those fabulous promises is found in the second half of Psalm 23:6.

Go to the Word: Read Psalm 23:6 again.

What long-lasting promise is offered to those who follow Jesus as their Shepherd?

God's intention is to live with us in proper relationship for all eternity. Why would He want this? Because He is a good God who desires good things for His creation. If we are His, we are promised to be with Him. And that is exactly where He wants us to be.

PRAYER FOR REST

As you finish up this study, take this Sabbath resting moment once again to spend time with the Lord, to speak with Him, to read His Word, and to learn to trust Him just a little more. Imagine all the goodness the Father wants to give you. Imagine peaceful pastures, cool water, and a cup overflowing with the love of the Lord. Challenge yourself not to give up taking these times to rest in the Lord, but to make this a daily practice.

Group Discussion

STARTER

Talk about your experience or understanding of Psalm 23 before this study. Has your understanding of it changed at all?

REVIEW

1. What types of daily needs do you find yourself worrying about? If you feel comfortable, share your answers. You might find that you aren't the only one.

2. How does trusting in the Good Shepherd alleviate worry in your life?

3. Why do you think God wants us to be honored and cared for? Why does He have a soft spot for those who are overlooked?

4. In Psalm 23:6, we see God wanting to live with us in relationship for all eternity. Why do you think He might want this?

5. How has this study of rest changed your view of God and your relationship with Him?

PRAYER FOR REST

Spend some time in silent prayer. Then let someone read Psalm 23, pausing after each verse, allowing time for group members to focus on the meaning of God's Word. Thank God for providing rest through His Word, through His promises, and through His faithful love.

Room to Reflect

LEADER GUIDE

Hello, Leaders!

Thank you for investing in the lives of the women around you! Whether this is your first time leading a Bible study or you've led many groups before, we appreciate the time and sacrifice you make for your group. We want to come alongside you and help you feel prepared to lead. Here you will find a starting-off point to help you prepare for your meeting times.

The group discussions can range from about 30–45 minutes if you are meeting in person. Below you will find a suggested outline for your group time, but feel free to tailor your time together to fit your needs.

GETTING STARTED TIPS

PRAY!!

As you are preparing to lead your group, prayer is key!! Spend time each week praying for the ladies in your group and praying that God will lead and direct your time.

FIND A LOCATION

Decide what works best for your group. Meeting at someone's house? At a coffee shop? In a local park? At a church? Online? Get some feedback. If the women in your group don't have the transportation, means, or the time to meet up somewhere— consider hosting an online Facebook group. We provide tips for how to do this at thrivemoms.com/community. If you have a really large group and can meet at your church, consider providing childcare.

PLAN AND PREPARE

Be very familiar with your material! Read through the material and make notes before your discussion time so you can make sure your time together flows smoothly.

FOLLOW UP

Take time during the week to follow up with the women in your group and check in on how they are doing. Remind them about meeting times, and encourage engagement within your group.

GROUP LEADING TIPS

BEFORE YOU MEET

Take some time to go through the week of material and make notes on anything that you may need to clarify deeper with your group. As a leader, you need to be prepared, so make sure you have answered every question, filled in every blank, and read all of the content. Go through all of the group discussion questions, answering each one and having questions picked out that you think will be good for your group. You can also use space on the discussion pages or the Room to Reflect pages to add questions or thoughts of your own.

Keep your mind and heart open to how the Lord leads your group. You may have someone come with a question, concern, or need that may take more time than you are prepared for. Your group time may not always look the way you think, so leave room for growth. Remember that your group members are getting into the material on their own too.

PREPARE

Helping to set a comfortable and inviting atmosphere for your group is a great way to start your meeting time each week.

This may be the only time during the week your women have away from their kids or (if kids are at the location) one of the few chances they have to partake in focused adult conversations that aren't all about their children or their work stress. You want them to walk in and feel a sense of peace and rest. Being a thoughtful host makes a huge difference in the atmosphere of your group and in your ability to connect with one another and the content.

Here are a few ways you can prepare for your group time:

- Pray over the room and each person attending.
- Minimize any distractions (remove sight and sound clutter as much as possible) and create a comfortable environment, with seating available for everyone. Your group will struggle to engage if they are uncomfortable and distracted.
- If you are hosting online—post ahead of time, welcoming them. Make sure your live video setup is comfortable and inviting, with clear sound and enough light.

WELCOME (10 Minutes)

As your group arrives, take some time to welcome each person and catch up briefly on what's happening in people's lives. Make any introductions or announcements you need to here. If drinks or snacks are available, invite everyone to get those before they find their seats.

DISCUSSION (20–30 Minutes)

Use the Starter question, if you wish, to begin the conversation. Sometimes, especially in groups where the members don't know one another well, it can be helpful to have a chance to talk about more everyday issues before diving into the spiritual discussion.

After a few people have responded to the Starter, move into the Review of the week's study by discussing the provided questions. If you are in the second week of the study or any week past that, it might also be helpful for you to briefly summarize the main points of the previous session (especially if some members haven't been able to make it to every meeting).

Allow people to share anything that stood out to them and to ask questions about any parts of the session they didn't understand. If you can, take notes about any specific needs or issues your group members mention so you can pray for those later.

PRAYER (5–10 Minutes)

After you complete your discussion time, build prayer into each group session. Prayer prompts are provided, or you may wish to spend some time going around and praying for the specific needs of your group members. Note pages are provided at the end of each session so people can jot down reminders of any needs they may want to continue praying over during the week. Check in with your women throughout the week and pray for them daily!

NOTES

WEEK THREE: WHY DO I FEEL SO EMPTY?

1. Kara-Kae James, *Mom Up: Thriving with Grace in the Chaos of Motherhood* (Colorado Springs: David C Cook, 2019), 31–32.

WEEK FOUR: BEING BETTER AT BEING BUSY

1. *Matthew Henry Commentary on the Whole Bible (Concise)*, "Ecclesiastes," Bible Study Tools, accessed May 31, 2019, www.biblestudytools.com/commentaries/matthew-henry-concise/ecclesiastes/3.html.

ABOUT THE AUTHORS

Kara-Kae James is a writer and encourager, passionate about seeing women's lives changed and impacted through the gospel. She is the founder and executive director of Thrive Moms, a ministry dedicated to seeing moms step out of survival mode and into the thriving, abundant life that God calls them to. She is also the author of the book *Mom Up: Thriving with Grace in the Chaos of Motherhood*.

Kara-Kae is married to her husband, Brook, and is a mom to four. She works daily to encourage women to reach their potential as moms and as daughters of Christ. She loves pouring into moms because she knows firsthand that many are struggling and in desperate need of a reminder that God loves us, and we are doing His holy work.

Ali Pedersen is a writer and pastor's wife who has a heart for bringing people together. She is the community director of Thrive Moms and works with women to find fellowship right where they are.

Ali is married to her husband, Nicolai, and is a mom to four girls. She spends her days creating resources for women, homeschooling her kiddos, and baking lots of cookies. She enjoys fostering community among women and creating deep relationships for the sake of the kingdom.

ℳ

EMPOWERING IMPERFECT MOMS WITH GOD'S PERFECT GRACE.

We invite you to join the Thrive Moms' Community—
a community of real women who are stepping out of
survival mode and into thriving, abundant life with Christ.
We focus on community, intentionality as moms,
finding our rest in the Lord, and embracing the
wonderfully chaotic moments of everyday life.
We continue to push each other deeper into God's Word
and know that we are better when we stand together.

JOIN US AT **THRIVEMOMS.COM** AND
DOWNLOAD THE **THRIVE MOMS APP**.

@thrivemoms

Elise Aileen Photography

 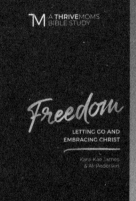